The Report of the
Task Force on Barriers to Women in the Public Service

BENEATH
THE
VENEER

VOL 3 UME

WHAT THE PEOPLE TOLD US

Canadian Cataloguing in Publication Data
Canada. Task Force on Barriers to Women in the Public Service

Beneath the veneer : the report of the Task Force on Barriers to Women in the Public Service

Issued also in French under title: Au-delà des apparences.
Contents: v. 1 Report and recommendations — v. 2 What the numbers told us — v. 3 What the people told us — v. 4 Annotated bibliography.
Includes bibliographical references.

ISBN 0-660-13583-3
DSS cat. no. BT22-19/3-1990E

1. Women in the civil service — Canada. 2. Equal pay for equal work — Canada. 3. Canada — Officials and employees. 4. Civil service — Canada. 5. Women — Employment — Canada. I. Title. II. Title: The report of the Task Force on Barriers to Women in the Public Service.

JL111.W6.C32 1990 Vol. 3   354.71001'04   C90-098617-4   65/23

© Minister of Supply and Services Canada 1990

Available in Canada through
Associated Bookstores and other booksellers

or by mail from

Canadian Government Publishing Centre
Supply and Services Canada
Ottawa, Canada K1A 0S9

Catalogue No. BT22-19/3-1990E
ISBN 0-660-13583-3

TABLE OF CONTENTS

Introduction

INTRODUCTION

As outlined in Chapter 1, "What We Did and How We Did It," the Task Force gathered a substantial amount of anecdotal material in the course of its research. The interviews with 70 pioneers and pathfinders alone produced over 2,000 pages of transcripts. Add to this the results of 90 structured interviews, over 50 "exit interviews" with former public servants, 15 case studies, 7,000 written responses to Question 47 of the questionnaire survey and the very high-quality briefs sent from departments, public service unions and other interested parties. Only a small portion of this material could be used in the body of the report itself and it was much too voluminous to publish in its entirety. The problem becomes obvious — how best to use this material?

The agreed solution was to produce a volume of anecdotal material that bore directly on the Task Force's Terms of Reference. Although the material has been edited for the sake of brevity, it has not been "censored" in any way. The results, therefore, represent a wide range of views and do not necessarily reflect the beliefs and opinions of the Task Force. No attempts have been made to verify the facts of any of the situations cited by the contributors.

Some of these sources were anonymous, others identified themselves to the Task Force but requested that their identity be protected. In such cases, details such as the names of departments have been omitted or are identified in broad terms only. In cases where the sources were not concerned with anonymity the details have been left unchanged.

The original material from which these excerpts have been drawn is lodged with the National Archives of Canada. It is subject to the provisions of the *Privacy Act* and the *Access to Information Act*. The responses to the Questionnaire Survey are subject to the *Statistics Act* and are in the custody of Statistics Canada.

The material in this volume is organized under three main sections.

Extracts from Briefs and Interviews
The material in this section is derived from the pioneer and pathfinder interviews, interviews with former public servants, structured interviews and briefs.

Selected Case Studies
These differ from interviews because those who participated in case studies were asked to agree that former and current colleagues and supervisors be interviewed to provide additional perspective and verify perceptions of events. In addition, case studies review an entire career rather than addressing the specific questions raised in the interviews.

To identify possible subjects for the case study project the Task Force consulted a number of sources, including the Advisory Committee of Deputy Ministers.

The 15 subjects who eventually agreed to participate represent a broad range of occupational groups and a variety of career patterns. There were 12 women and 3 men chosen from departments of various sizes, many with both head-quarters and regional experience. Some of the subjects have stayed in one department for their entire career, others have moved extensively. All of the subjects have at least ten years of federal public service experience (some have also worked in the private sector) and entered at a low or entry level. Some of the subjects have never been promoted, others advanced rapidly, still others have had a more moderate progression.

The interviews were carried out on behalf of the Task Force by Price Waterhouse. The subjects were asked to "talk about" their careers in a very open-ended fashion, then specific areas were followed up in detail. These included concerns faced at key points in their career, specific skills or individuals who facilitated progression, approaches to balancing work and personal life, etc.

Each subject was also asked to identify a number of former colleagues, supervisors, and co-workers from various points in their careers. These individuals were interviewed in a more structured manner, focusing on incidents or issues in the subject's career with which they were familiar. Both subjects and colleagues were asked to provide suggestions to improve the areas under discussion. No attempt has been made to resolve differences of opinion or varying perspectives. Rather, the comments were allowed to speak for themselves.

Four illustrative Case Studies are reproduced in this volume.

Selected Comments from the Questionnaire Survey
Question 47 of the questionnaire survey asked respondents "Do you have any further comments on the advancement of men and women in the federal public service?" Some 7,000 respondents, over 60% of all respondents, chose to write additional views. A cross-section of typical replies, selected by Statistics Canada, is included in this volume.

EXTRACTS FROM
BRIEFS
AND
INTERVIEWS

SECTION 1
Attitudes

(1) STEREOTYPING

If a woman answers the phone it is assumed that she is a secretary.

$\cdot\ \cdot\ \cdot\ \cdot\ \cdot$

(There is an assumption that) women aren't able to travel.

$\cdot\ \cdot\ \cdot\ \cdot\ \cdot$

(There is a feeling that) women can't handle money. The FI and the Audit categories have few women.

$\cdot\ \cdot\ \cdot\ \cdot\ \cdot$

Women don't advance because they aren't ambitious and they think differently than men. If you were married, I think that you would find that men think differently than women.

$\cdot\ \cdot\ \cdot\ \cdot\ \cdot$

I took extra training at night which was difficult as I had two small children and was pregnant with my third. With this course in gerontology and my certified nursing assistant experience, I was more than qualified to be a WP-2 Counsellor. I competed and always came second. The men who came first had no more, usually less, training. Coming second meant my name was put on an eligible list, but acting appointments were given to two males instead of myself. I was told by my supervisor that it would be hard for me to travel, having young children, and with winter conditions. I finally put in a grievance and was offered an acting position. The door to a permanent position was not offered. I only received a permanent position by applying to (another office several hours drive away.)

$\cdot\ \cdot\ \cdot\ \cdot\ \cdot$

(I was told) if you are not happy, you should spend more time at home with your child.

$\cdot\ \cdot\ \cdot\ \cdot\ \cdot$

> *Women don't advance because they aren't ambitious and they think differently than men.*

All officers leaving a post were given gifts except the wife (full-time government employee) of a working couple. It was considered that the gift to the husband "covered" them both as employees.

· · · · ·

My job is Informatics Officer. I offer user support for informatics software and computer hardware, as well as administer the office automation system. I am often trying to help one of the men on the floor, but am pushed out of the way or asked ridiculous questions such as "Check the dip switches. Do you know what a dip switch is?" This is my job. I am fully qualified to perform this job and I resent having some man assume that because I am female I don't understand the mechanics of the equipment involved.

· · · · ·

I was told by my supervisor that it would be hard for me to travel.

Career-oriented women who remove themselves from the workplace for periods of time to deliver babies and/or nurture infants are obviously putting themselves at a competitive disadvantage with men. This is surely an obvious consideration in promoting a woman of child-bearing years.

(Part-time work) appeals to a lot of married women with families ... All they want is a supplementary income to provide a few luxuries they would otherwise have to live without.

(Women who have been out of the work force raising children) are not career oriented but want as few responsibilities and pressures as possible and are content to earn a nice little supplementary income.

· · · · ·

I obtained my diploma in Naval Architecture ... graduating at the top of my class. I went to an interview ... and was interviewed by a panel of four people. I found the vein of questioning and the delivery highly insulting. For example: "Do electronics scare you?" "Do power tools or hand tools scare you?" "Are you afraid to get dirty?" "Would you be offended if (co-workers) swore while you were around and how would you handle it?"

I had spent the previous summer in an electronics shop at the Institute for Marine Dynamics and had run my own test project. Both facts were clearly outlined on my CV.

I learned afterwards from one of my referees that the reason I was turned down was that the supervisor flatly refused to work with a woman.

One of the projects involved working extremely long hours, sometimes around the clock, with no recompense at all. During the course of the job the senior officer commented twice to me that "You should be home having babies, cleaning the kitchen and cooking supper for your husband."

· · · · ·

When I was first applying for the job one of the guys asked me if I knew what job I was applying for. I said "Yes, a firefighter." He asked me if I was sure I wanted to apply for it and I answered "Yes, it seems like a good job and I think I am qualified for it." He replied that it wasn't really a woman's type of job, and I said, "Too bad."

· · · · ·

I walked in and said, "Hi, I'm here, — let's get started, I want to learn." They took me for a walk around and I could just feel that everybody was waiting for me to start moving furniture and putting drapes up — you know, "women things."

· · · · ·

About 15 or 16 years ago there were no women STS-03s. There were women packers and helpers in the warehouse depot, but it was deemed that women couldn't do the job, they couldn't do the lifting, they'd be off two or three days a month.

· · · · ·

I was dealing with men like my father, who had been brought up with women having a traditional role. There was resentment and there was "Oh well, let's watch this silly broad fall on her face, because we all know that no woman can do our job." But it was never outright hostile, and at that point I was still in a non-threatening area. I was new, I was a woman, and everybody was standing back and watching every move I made.

· · · · ·

In 1972 or 1973 a competition went up that was the first open competition where women could participate. It stated right there "Women can apply." At the time I was a clerk and I really didn't like what I was doing. When I was in the air force I had been on the floor and had been the stores person. So I applied and much to the horror of a lot of the men here, I placed 14th or 15th out of 85. It was almost as if I had taken off all my clothes and marched stark naked around the depot. The reaction that people had was "Oh my God! A woman!" This really rocked this place right down to the foundations.

· · · · ·

If you are a woman, management fears that you are going to leave to have a baby and take time off. For seven years I was queried on this during performance appraisals.

· · · · ·

If you are not happy, you should spend more time at home with your child.

It is still assumed that women are primarily responsible for child care, and therefore if a woman has children her ability to work overtime, travel, transfer, etc. will be more limited than a man's.

· · · · ·

What gets in the way? Ignorance and attitudes of those in a position to influence advancement. For example, some personnel officers believe that secretaries and librarians are interchangeable; they are unaware of the qualifications required to be a librarian. Librarians have a real problem promoting themselves as a professional group — the commonly held perception is that "librarians are clerks who stamp books."

· · · · ·

There are different reactions at work between when a man calls in to say he has to stay home with a sick child versus when a woman calls in for the same reason. For the man, the comment is something like: "It is too bad the man's wife cannot stay home with the child" whereas this leave is frowned upon when the woman is absent.

· · · · ·

Some managers seem to think that once an individual has been in a clerical position that person cannot be considered for an officer position. The individual is branded. There is a stigma in being identified as a clerk.

· · · · ·

Jobs are still stereotyped. Physically demanding jobs are still seen as male, and secretarial/clerical jobs are seen as women's work. The degree to which this applies varies from department to department.

· · · · ·

Men consider middle-management jobs to be "male" jobs, and are more likely to appoint other men into acting positions in order to develop them and make them more able to win the competition. Excuses are that women can't do budgets; can't supervise men; can't make tough decisions. That women make emotional decisions.

· · · · ·

In some departments women at meetings are still expected to bring coffee, go for photocopies, etc., regardless of the level of their positions.

· · · · ·

Another barrier is the way people see you. Because I'm a female manager people expect to see me a certain way. They expect me to act a certain way and when I don't they're confused. I think they expect me to be more permissive. They expect me to be a little more sympathetic. It doesn't mean that I'm not sympathetic, but I do recognize that people have to work 37 hours a week. That's what they're getting paid for.

· · · · ·

When I came into the public service, women in management positions were unheard of. Women in non-traditional roles were especially unheard of. I recall working on a program that involved monthly visits to a dairy farm. I remember a woman applying for that job. There was absolute shock that a woman would even want that job. There was a tremendous amount of concern that the diary farmers that she visited would not welcome her because she was a woman. I was in a position that had a bit of influence over decisions like that so I asked questions like, "Why not?" and "What's wrong with this?" Anyway, she was hired and it was quite a surprise to a lot of people. I think we only had one complaint and that was from a dairy farmer who said that a woman's place was not in a dairy barn. So for women who wanted to get into non-traditional jobs there were definitely barriers. But these barriers were attitudes. A lot of the attitude was protectionist. For example, men who felt that they wouldn't want their sister or mother doing that. I'm talking about heavier jobs, particularly in labour.

· · · · ·

It was really important for me to get this one position, so I studied and studied. I did very well at the try-outs and a lot of people came up to me afterward and told me that I had done very well. However, it was all males and all economists who ended up getting the positions. So, I swallowed my pride and asked them what I could have done better. I reasoned that I could not have done as good as I thought, or else I would have got it. So, I went up to the Chief of Training, who happened to be a woman, and asked her how I could have done better. She told me that I was magnificent and that I couldn't have done better. But, she said that I was married, I had a small child and therefore I wouldn't be able to travel. They didn't even ask me if I could travel. My mother lived with me at that time and she could look after my child while I was out. But she didn't even ask me.

· · · · ·

We'd say, "Well we're looking at the Weapons Technologists and the demands of their jobs..." and they'd say, "Are you here to get women in our trade?" and because I'm a woman, usually the only one, there were always comments like "Are you one of those women's libbers?"

(2) PATRONIZING
(I had a) straight-A Master's degree and at Transport they patted me on the head.

· · · · ·

I had a straight-A Master's degree and at Transport they patted me on the head.

Our Regional Chief, for example, usually greets me with a smile and a big "Hello" — but has emphatically stated ... that women shouldn't be doing this kind of work and that he didn't want any female technicians hired. To the Deputy Minister, to whom I was proudly introduced as the only female technician in our outfit, he said "If we could find more like (her), we'd hire a dozen!"

. . . . .

The clerks are called "cutie" or "sweetie."

. . . . .

After I had waited a year to get into a pre-apprenticeship course my apprenticeship counsellor, with whom I had been dealing all along, neglected to tell me that the course start date had changed. When I went in he said, "Oh, gee, I am sorry but that course started two weeks ago." I think it was because he wouldn't take me seriously.

. . . . .

In my first year here, we had an international statistical evening. I was the local organizer of the thing, and to my absolute astonishment I discovered that I had been assigned to arrange the women's program.

. . . . .

I was talking to a grade 7 class and I had one boy who kept saying, "What a joke" or "Women or girls can't be firefighters." I said that I have been doing it for 12 years so I guess girls can be firefighters. He just shrugged his shoulders and, you know, kind of slouched back in his seat. He wasn't going to listen to any of this garbage.

. . . . .

In an interview with External Affairs, I was told "You would make a better wife of an ambassador than an ambassador."

. . . . .

I remember when I started working for the military and people called me "Dear." I don't like to be called "Dear."

. . . . .

Just yesterday I heard one of the 55-year-old men saying, " My girl." "Excuse me" I feel like yelling "Do you have your daughter working here?"

. . . . .

When I started, the attitudes of superiors were somewhat paternalistic. I think to some extent my boss sees me as the one Division Chief who will do what he wants me to do. I will be good, the good girl.

. . . . .

My boss here has been very supportive of me. I think to some extent, I am very often treated like somebody's daughter, you know, not just by my boss, but by the public service in general. "We need to look after you."

· · · · ·

I'm sometimes treated like they would treat their wives and I hate to say that because I don't want to diminish the role of their wife or anything, but that's very annoying.

· · · · ·

When we were dropped off to do some work the pilot would hang around and not want to leave because he just didn't feel right about leaving two women with just a tent out on a bald hillside at 35 below.

· · · · ·

There's a scientist who's a bit of a mentor. He's older and I consider him to be a friend, but I will do something and he will say, "Good girl." He will ask my opinion on things and doesn't consider me an idiot, but I'm the same age as his daughter and that's the way he treats me.

· · · · ·

When I hear stories about how women are being pampered, etc., I always say that women are often not given the same tasks as men on the job because the men don't think the women can do them. The women are perfectly willing and able but aren't given the chance. So they are being forcibly pampered.

I'm the same age as his daughter and that's the way he treats me.

(3) UNDERVALUING

If you are a secretary or a clerk in the public service you are always seen as that and it's hard to break the barrier. If you go outside of government, employers look at you as a person with capabilities. They look at your performance and your background and they give you a chance.

· · · · ·

Men do not recognize secretarial skills of organizing and managing people and information. They tend to think of secretarial work as typing and filing.

· · · · ·

I did have enough sense to use my first initial on my publications. One scientist showed surprise on finding that I was the author of a certain article and remarked, "Gee, if I'd known that, I wouldn't have read the paper."

· · · · ·

I was the logical person for the job, but I was told: "Sorry, we need a man with experience for that job." The man they put into the job blew it, and three months later I was seconded to it.

· · · · ·

A man had been doing the job previously, then they offered me the job, but at one level lower. I was told that he needed the money because he had a family.

· · · · ·

When I took over the job there had been a man there before me, and he had the title of "director." When I got in there I was told "It's no longer a director's job."

· · · · ·

For about a year I had been told I'd be getting a promotion. After I left, the person who replaced me was a man, and he came in at a higher level than me. You get a pretty clear message from the public service when these things happen.

· · · · ·

As a certified nursing assistant, although low with respect to pay, there were high rewards in giving comfort to the sick. As a clerk, there were quotas — the reward for reaching them was to have them increased. Supervisors and managers barely acknowledged that a clerk or steno existed.

· · · · ·

Supervisors and managers barely acknowledged that a clerk or steno existed.

... men were given grooming opportunities for bigger and better things: women were labelled as support or admin.

· · · · ·

(When it comes to office space), it is left to the support staff to contend with noise, constant people traffic, disruptions and the like within their space, plus the control of files, office supplies, storage, public reception and many more obstacles, all the while staff/managers enjoy offices offering window views, quietness, confidentiality and individual control. This reinforces my belief that women will always be required to overcome obstacles in the workplace as long as managers believe that the classification/salary of the individual determines the space they receive.

· · · · ·

There is a freeze within Transport Canada for hiring support staff. Any number of engineers or technical staff can be hired, but there is not enough support staff to handle the work generated by these people. Of 118 employees (in the division), there are 100 men and 18 women. Seven of these women are involved in the reorganization of the admin-istration section, eight are secretaries with anywhere from 10-25 men to work for, two are clerks and one is a low-level technical inspector.

· · · · ·

If a woman runs into a situation where there is a bias, a prejudice against her, then she is in a really tough spot. She is only going to be seen as an administrative assistant.

· · · · ·

I still meet men in their forties and fifties who are astonished by the level of my capabilities on the job. Some have made it clear their astonishment is because I'm a woman.

· · · · ·

I took the job at the Women's Bureau and it was a very rewarding experience because I was marketing the talents of very qualified, competent women. I was faced with the tokenism of, "We'll take her because we have to." My response? "Look, we're not marketing junk here. This isn't a meat market. This isn't a stale roast. This is an excellent resource."

· · · · ·

Brains are passed out randomly, and 50% of them land up in women's heads. Why would you limit yourself to half of the supply, and take the bottom of that half to fill your positions, when you could have the top of the other half?

· · · · ·

I asked my Director at that time if I could have a transfer and he was willing to facilitate it. However, the Regional Director would not agree — he said that because I was a woman neither the unions nor the other directors would take me seriously. I was insulted because I knew that I could do the work, and that the person they had hired was not competent.

· · · · ·

I know damn well that if I were ever to leave and they put a man in here they'd say, "God, we've lost one hell of a resource." But they don't know what they've got until it's gone.

· · · · ·

I have not observed a male colleague having to undergo this same struggle for recognition in the workplace, but I am tired and I don't want to do it anymore.

(4) SCEPTICISM
... female officers are often not accorded the same credibility and respect as their male colleagues.

· · · · ·

Brains are passed out randomly, and 50% of them land up in women's heads.

I found that as a woman, one had to be even more careful because people, particularly men, sat in judgement to make them feel that they hadn't proven any records.

· · · · ·

As a construction carpenter you go on new jobs all the time and so you are not working with the same crew of people with whom you have built up relationships over a period of time. So every time everybody is going to ask, "Huh, what is she doing here?" "Am I going to have to carry her boards?" "Am I going to have to do her work?" or "What is she after anyway, sex?" Every single time you have to prove yourself. Thankfully that's not hard, but there is that first two-week period where everybody is watching you.

· · · · ·

The way it sounds is: everything I've applied for I've gotten. That's not true. There have been cases of course where I haven't. But when I have gotten them, I've suffered in having to prove myself all over again. Each and every time.

· · · · ·

Women have to prove their excellence over and over as they move from one job to another while men take their credentials with them.

· · · · ·

There's something about women not being able to make it because they are competent. There's a perception that we've only made it because we knew somebody. What do we do about that? I mean, I've had to fight that constantly in my career.

· · · · ·

I see women in responsible positions who want to be perfect. Women tend to feel that they have to do a little bit more and make sure it's perfect. It's because we're expecting to be judged all the time.

· · · · ·

You cannot afford to leave an "i" undotted or a "t" uncrossed because every little chink, every little careless word, written or spoken, is a good reason to say you are less than competent.

· · · · ·

I think I sometimes overdo it, drive my own people crazy with my level of productivity. But if a woman is doing something for the first time, like being deputy minister of this department, people watch for you to trip and they're not tolerant if you do. The pressure is great. If you're male, it's a hot seat, but it's accepted that a woman can't do the job.

· · · · ·

Every little chink, every little careless word, is a good reason to say you are less than competent.

Women do have to work harder. But quite often the expectations of what you can achieve are so low that when you do an outstanding or even reasonable job, people are amazed.

· · · · ·

When I'm looking for a director, I see some very competent scientists, female scientists and I fall into the trap of saying, well, has she ever managed anything before? However, quite often, while women have not managed, they have had to use all the talent you need to be a good manager, but in the role of co-ordinating, establishing and building records. But we tend to look for the practical experience of managing large groups of people. I'm not sure we do the same thing with men.

· · · · ·

It is frankly easier to assign a woman to a job for which she is over-qualified than to persuade a supervisor to accept her in an assignment where she has the qualifications and potential but is unknown or untested in that area of the department's work.

· · · · ·

If you push a female candidate on male managers you're not helping her. You must make sure that the woman is visible and that she has a heavy workload, because a normal workload will not impress anyone.

· · · · ·

I've also found that women think that to win a job competition and be promoted to a new job, they must know all about it. Men are different. Men get a new job and then go on to learn what the new job is all about. So the expectations that women create for themselves makes life more difficult for them. Even my best male managers, who I know really want to give women a chance, still have great difficulty. The women they pick for jobs have proven track records — a very, very high ratio of delivery all the time. These are the women who finally are able to make it to the senior levels.

· · · · ·

Lack of supervisory experience really hurts a woman in the executive ranks. Somehow we can see a man with an English degree who has never supervised as an executive, but we can't see a woman the same way. It seems that it is critical for women to have had the actual experience, while we will say of a man "Well, you know, he hasn't supervised anybody, but we know he can."

· · · · ·

You must make sure that the woman has a heavy workload, because a normal workload will not impress anyone.

The one woman instructor that had been there had been deemed unsuccessful. I said, "What did you base your judgement on?" and they answered "Well she couldn't teach," I said "Had she ever been allowed to teach?" and they said "No, we knew she couldn't teach."

· · · · ·

When I was climbing the totem pole, my biggest problem was that the people I worked for didn't understand me. It wasn't that I am not articulate or I am weird; I would be sitting in a meeting, the only woman, and we would be discussing something. I would put forward a point of view but it would not be heard; a man would present that same point, saying, "As she was saying ...," and then it would become something for the record. When I said it, the person in the chair would not recognize me or hear what I said. I don't know what the hell they saw when they looked at me, really.

· · · · ·

I go to meetings and if I make a statement or something I find it's never taken at face value right off the bat. It has to be discussed 10 or 15 times until one of the men will say about the same thing — all of the sudden it's a great idea.

(5) HOSTILITY

I was told by somebody quite high up that he didn't know why I had got the position because he knew that I couldn't do half the jobs that I would be asked to, and I told him "Well, you'd be surprised at what I can do." He said "Oh well, first time you are out unloading trucks you'll come crying to get changed around." So of course when I was down there I realized that whatever came up no matter how dirty, no matter how icky, I pretty well had to do it and not make any bones about it.

· · · · ·

I did encounter hostility. There was one gentleman who was an STS-3 and of the old school and I went to ask him why he did it this way, and he said, "You are the STS-4, you should know." We had another guy who hated women. He and I butted heads quite often. But after I was in that area for about three or four years, the very person who had said he didn't want me, when he left he asked me if I would go with him. There were times I could tell men were egging me on to see how I would react. I think it helped that they found out that I wasn't scared of taking disciplinary action against a man.

· · · · ·

In 1981 I accepted a position as a technician, because the section head who interviewed me told me that with my qualifications I could advance to the professional level. I worked hard for two years and received good evaluations. I then approached the section head, only to find that things had now changed. He informed me that I now could not expect to move into the professional group without a Ph.D.

I took a two-year leave of absence without pay to return to university, and was promised, in writing, a professional position on my return. I went to university and completed most of my Ph.D. requirements, receiving my degree in 1987.

When I returned to work it was as if I had the plague. Not only did I not receive a professional position, I was screened out of a competition and not allowed to compete.

I continued to work as a technician, and was awarded a post-doctoral fellowship. After much debate, I was given a two-year leave of absence to undertake this project at a sister establishment to that where I worked. In less than 18 months, I put together a lab, a project director and produced two publications. At the end of the two-year period, I was given a satisfactory evaluation but with a poor personal suitability rating, based on malicious, untrue and contrived statements.

When I returned to my technician position, I was then told that due to this evaluation I would have to prove myself once again before I could be considered for a professional position.

For the last eight years I have worked hard to advance myself and followed all of management's suggestions, only to have the rug pulled out from under my feet each time. I am presently at my wit's end with little confidence or self-esteem left.

· · · · ·

Later on I won a competition for an STS-4, and I was due to move up to my new area, and a friend came to me and said "You know, I don't really want to see you go up there because you are getting into a really hostile environment." When I asked him what he meant he said "Well, a statement was made by a certain person quite high up in that work centre that he doesn't want women coming in and messing the place up. You are really going to have a lot of hostility." And I said, "Well, it's too late now, I got the job I want." There were two men — one that would be my equal and one that would be my boss — who did not want me.

· · · · ·

Before I came, they said, "There is a woman coming from Western Region." "You know bloody well she's a pilot." "Yeah, I know. I hear she's a real bitch."

· · · · ·

I started to encounter major hostility from co-workers when I started to try and advance. When I tried for an STS-4, which is first-level supervisory in the warehouse, I did very well for a first-timer, I think I placed third or fourth on the list. There was an appeal launched against me by one of my co-workers. What it boiled down to was a woman could not possibly be intelligent enough to do this, she must have cheated. At the appeal board, a lot of things came up, and I was quite angry and I said "If I were a man this appeal would have never been launched." You should have seen the backpeddling by the lawyer of the guy that appealed. "No, no, we never said that." I said, "Yes, you did. You didn't say it in words, but it is there."

· · · · ·

One guy in the Yukon got me mad. He wanted to know what the hell I thought I was trying to prove, that this isn't fun up here, this isn't summer camp, this is dangerous stuff. He was a weird macho guy; if a woman could do it, it became less dramatic.

· · · · ·

There are barriers that come from the attitudes of your colleagues. If you are a competitive woman you will have one of two responses. Some male colleagues are very enthusiastic and think this is rather fun and you are treated like one of the guys. Others regard you as an undue threat.

· · · · ·

(I was told) "everyone in the office is afraid of you: go to the private sector where your competence, energy and motivation can be better used."

· · · · ·

Male supervisors are more threatened by women than female supervisors. Men are used to being threatened by other men and they have the locker-room experience to deal with this. However, they are not accustomed to being threatened by women in a professional sense.

· · · · ·

The old boys' club exists. That is, men support each other as mentors. Many women who entered the service in recent years have a much higher educational level than some of their co-workers who have years in the service, yet we are viewed with contempt, and as a threat by our male counterparts.

· · · · ·

Men are not accustomed to being threatened by women in a professional sense.

Other public servants' attitudes towards you can be a problem. If you are female, unusual, entrepreneurial, and a "yes" response person, then you may encounter resistance. There is an attitude that "if we must have women, then let's have someone who isn't noisy or in an important department." There are three waves of male resistance — the older Old Boys' Club; the contemporary movers who view women as competition; and the future wave of neo-conservative university graduates. The resistance is continuous.

. . . . .

The greatest obstacle to promotion is people; insecure men who can't cope with positiveness and energy. It drives them crazy. Fortunately I haven't run into too many of them. This is especially troublesome when one boss leaves and another comes. If he is threatened, you need to leave as he can kill you by undermining you in front of your staff, poor appraisals, etc. This situation is always scary. Another barrier for women is sexuality. Women are kidding themselves if they think it is not there. I had a boss who was wonderful; we would chat away; then after a year he made a pass. I left because it added a dimension to the work environment that was difficult to deal with.

. . . . .

Because I work in a male dominated field, the problems have to do with gender: attitudes of males. They ask: "What are we going to do with you? Are you going to be a member of the boys' club or are you going to be yourself?" Then there are the rumours: "We know how she got there." Some men (insecure ones) are very threatened by competent women working for them.

. . . . .

The management style in my department is largely hypocritical in that the spoken word is different from what actually happens. The management style of men toward women is strange. Men don't know how to deal with women. They come on to women managers, patronize them, feel uncomfortable or clam up. Very few act in a normal way. There's a lot more of this type of behaviour from men than I expected, especially at the executive level, more so than at the SM level. Strong men do not know how to deal with strong women. Senior managers in general have problems with people close to them in their hierarchy as opposed to having no problems with their subordinates.

. . . . .

When my boss was transferred, my new supervisor's attitudes to women were out of the Ark. In his first conversation with me he asked me when I was moving back to Ottawa. I knew then that I should look for another job. When appointed, this man inherited the highest percentage of female managers and supervisors in departmental regional offices across Canada. They have all left for other jobs. Fortunately, this is the only time in my 20+ years in the public service that I have had an experience of this type.

· · · · ·

On one woman's first day on the job one of her colleagues came into her office and without introducing himself, said "I don't care for women in this business" and walked out. Needless to say, the rest of the team were more welcoming.

· · · · ·

It was not the usual situation where a woman has to be twice as good. This woman was three times as good as the other candidates. Nevertheless, some of the senior male scientists sought to undercut her qualifications. Finally I had to assert my influence on the staffing decision. I realize that I will have to be very careful to "bring her into the fold" so that the diehards do not exclude her from the informal network. I'm confident that the younger scientists, at least, will accept her expertise in a demanding area.

· · · · ·

The directorate that I worked in had about 130 employees and when there was a full management meeting (about 30 of us) I would be the only woman. There wasn't another female manager. When the DG first announced that I would be working there, the reaction was like, "Oh Jesus, that'll be difficult to manage" and "I'm not working for any goddamn female, that's just not gonna work, forget it." So, at first they were very nervous and stiff with me.

· · · · ·

Men on the whole, even if they liked you, would still decide that their bread was buttered on the other side. They had no interest in equality at all when it came down to a choice. However, if they were not involved in something competitive then their attitude was very supportive.

· · · · ·

I'm an acting supervisor now. I supervise the same men who were working with me before. Only two of the original group is still with me; the others all left. At first there was a lot of hard feeling, they

My new supervisor's attitudes to women were out of the Ark.

didn't want to talk to me or associate with me. One of the guys said that he would never take orders from a woman boss. But they did what they were told, though they might have a sarcastic remark.

· · · · ·

The most difficult problem I face as a manager is managing a couple of men in the organization, who really don't want to be managed by a woman. It causes me untold, undue stress.

· · · · ·

As soon as you step out into supervisory capacities the attitude changes completely. They don't want to accept you in that role.

· · · · ·

I was the boss of the field crew and the only problem was one fellow who was older. He had his forestry diploma and was a carpenter by trade. He didn't like taking orders from a woman.

· · · · ·

If two female officers are discussing a problem in the corridor, as frequently happens, males who pass often cannot resist making a comment about this, as if they suspect a conspiracy.

· · · · ·

I get sort of an underlying feeling of support but then I also sometimes feel that they resent me. You know, they must think that it must be nice to get all of this time off (maternity leave). There is someone else at work that has taken a lot of sick time off with a bad back and a bad knee and a bunch of other stuff. I am being likened to him and I don't like that at all because as far as I am concerned somebody who is taking advantage of the system is not like someone who is taking what is in place for working mothers.

· · · · ·

Since I came back from maternity leave there have been some negative feelings, you know, snide comments about how nice it is to have me back at work after all that time off.

· · · · ·

But the anti-female ones ... some of them said they had no objection to a woman being appointed if the Prime Minister wanted to make such a gesture but why did they have to be the victims of this.

(6) WOMEN'S OWN ATTITUDES

There are definitely cases in which a woman has somehow managed to prevent another woman from advancing and gaining knowledge to further her goals and ambitions.

· · · · ·

I was right royally snubbed because I had gone out of my home to take a job.

(When I first entered the work force) I was the outcast as far as women were concerned. In fact, I was right royally snubbed because I had gone out of my home to take a job.

• • • • •

I was in my office talking to my Director when a staff member walked by with her toddler. She was unable to leave her child with day-care and so she had to bring her to work with her. The Director I was talking to thought this was ridiculous. I was horrified by her attitude, especially as she came from the Status of Women. She had enough money to pay for a good day-care centre, but this woman was a single parent on an IS-3 salary and was having a hard time paying for day-care.

• • • • •

Some others seem to feel that it's more appropriate not to help women. They may even disparage their female colleagues, perhaps to deny their membership in their sex and enhance their self-perception of having "made it" solely by their own efforts.

• • • • •

Women, for instance, through their upbringing and culture, tend on the whole to be more modest than many of their male colleagues about their achievements. They tend to be overly modest in reporting their accomplishments, or at least, less prone to exaggerate. More seriously, in the cases where officers write part or all of their own appraisals, (an all too frequent occurrence), women tend to under-rate themselves.

• • • • •

A woman's greatest barrier is lack of confidence in herself. We are new to the work force, and our role models are our mothers. We weren't groomed for the idea that we might be a plumber or a brain surgeon. When I look for a role model, there isn't one. I am on my own. When my daughter looks at her mother and her father she sees both bring home the bacon. She doesn't have any preconceived notions about what she should or should not do. The problem that most women have is they don't have clear, defined role models on how to behave.

• • • • •

Women being interviewed want to emphasize what they have done before because they are not at all comfortable in selling themselves.

• • • • •

How you get one assignment from the next has a lot to do with how you sell yourself and how you make yourself known. I think women find it difficult to pull the strings.

• • • • •

My male colleagues are not necessarily aggressive but they know they are doing well and they feel confident when they speak to senior management. When they speak with authority it inspires confidence. Sometimes I think that women lack this self-confidence. They tend to be more respectful of the line of authority. I remember I was quite respectful of the line of authority when I started. I think men taught themselves better than women.

. . . . .

The senior level of the public service is really a political world. It's a political battle and you have to be an inside player to get around. Information is gold; information is power. If you want to play the game successfully you must be an insider. Perhaps it is easier for a man to be an insider. I think women are naturally outsiders, so it is more difficult to become an insider, to be part of a network. I think women tend to be a little more shy. I can see that some women find it difficult to enter this inner circle. There is the perception that they are not wanted. And certainly men are not going out of their way to bring women in.

. . . . .

I make clocks at home but I don't have any skills.

Women don't have the confidence, personal confidence, that they can do the work. This one woman said, "Well, I make clocks at home but I don't have any skills." We see what we do as a hobby or something else! Not as an employable skill. So I think in terms of personal barriers, you know, like socialization or a lack of self-esteem or self-confidence.

. . . . .

You always seem to be able to get around if you are visible and assertive, but there are very competent women who don't have that kind of personality, who just can't advertise themselves ... You really have to do that in the Government, because the results of your work are not immediately apparent, and the programs carry on for years. In our branch, individuals tend to work alone, so it's quite possible that only one other person, who may be someplace else, really knows the extent of what you do.

. . . . .

I don't think I'd be where I am today if I had sat back in the woods. Women themselves have to be a little more assertive and they have to prove themselves.

. . . . .

SECTION 2
Corporate Culture

I cannot see myself on this fishing trip with 14 men.

(1) OLD BOYS' NETWORK

(Told by her manager, when refused an acting appointment in favour of an older but less experienced man) "After all, us older fellows must stick together and look after each other."

· · · · ·

Guys feel more socially at ease with guys ... Men enjoy having me work on special projects because I am capable, but they won't hire me because they can't relate to me on a day-to-day basis.

· · · · ·

I cannot network through golf tournaments, I don't play golf. And I know that a lot of business is done that way — that has hampered me. But I recognize that I don't want to play golf!

· · · · ·

The fact is that when the guys go for lunch things get done and a lot of friendships get made. Women don't have that sort of networking.

· · · · ·

My male staff here all play ball together. They have a poker club every month! Only guys! And I've told them that I was going to play with them. But it's been kind of a joke: "Oh well, sure, come!" but it would be hell if I showed up. They'd faint!

· · · · ·

I'm on a board of directors and they always have a fishing trip the weekend before the annual meeting. I cannot see myself on this fishing trip with 14 men. But, somewhere over the course of this fishing trip they are going to be talking about the annual meeting and the strategies to approach various things.

· · · · ·

Gender harassment — making fun of women — does make women uncomfortable. I don't know if you call it harassment or not, it depends on the man. Sometimes when you're in a meeting with other men you get the distinct impression that you're putting a lid on any fun that they might have. You feel you're putting a damper on everything. Also, there are the discussions that take place after hours, at the bars. If there is a bunch of guys and only one woman, you don't go most of the time.

. . . . .

I never tried to be one of the boys. I didn't like the tough talk; I felt that if I stayed in my corner they couldn't bring me down to their level. I know men talk like that; even my husband talks like that, but not at home.

. . . . .

(Re a teacher who didn't try to stop on-going harassment) He wanted to be one of the guys, he wanted to be liked by the guys in the class and so the wolf-pack mentality was allowed to pervade the situation. He allowed it because he really didn't know how else to handle it.

. . . . .

Another time I was nominated for a management course. No woman had ever gone on this course. They told me that I could not go because they did not have separate washroom facilities and they didn't think it would work. So, my director, who was a tremendous guy, shouted and screamed at them and I shouted and screamed. They responded by saying that the men on the course could not really talk, the way men like to talk, if a woman was there. If I was there it would affect the kind of language they like to use. Finally I was told that I could go. But I could not stay in the residence; I had to commute to the course every day. But when it came time for me to get the money for commuting they would not pay for it. They told me that I would have to prove that it was necessary for me to commute every day. They make me commute and I have to prove it. They would not try that kind of stuff with a man.

. . . . .

During the time I spent as an assistant controller learning the ropes I was accepted. When other women started coming they were strangers and all of a sudden they were not as accepted. It was funny because Transport Canada did a study because they were having difficulty attracting women into this field because the rumor was that things were bad for them. Transport went around the country and asked controllers how they felt about having female controllers on board and

If there is a bunch of guys and only one woman, you don't go most of the time.

the general opinion at the time was that women didn't belong. It was a man's job. Then they would quote my name and those being interviewed would say, "Oh her? She's different." You see you had to be one of the boys. I was lucky! I was the one that got accepted here.

· · · · ·

I have never had a boss whose wife worked outside the home. Men's homes are controlled by women and the nature of his home environment controls whether a man comes to work belligerent or very happy. I wish my bosses had been married to women who worked at least part-time; they would have brought that to their homes. I have always been the one that had to bend, had to find a way of working within this situation. If the people at the top could be more aware, more of us would have made it up the ladder. Not everybody can be slapped on the face repeatedly and still keep coming back for more.

· · · · ·

The first thing the Government did was to take their documentation and change it to his/her, he/she, but meanwhile it's still a male world. There's always that little thing in there that's hidden that you a woman can identify and if you were going to stop them and tap them on the shoulder they'd say "You're crazy, you're exaggerating, you're one of those feminists who is trying to push women ahead." It's always there.

· · · · ·

I had a lot of good competent women scientists here, but they were all on contract. Male managers were telling me that women scientists just do not exist, that the talent is just not there. I discovered that I have 12 women scientists that have been working here on contract for two or three years and have been assessed as Fully Satisfactory or Superior. Once we discovered that, we made a submission to the Public Service Commission and we were able to get special permission to appoint these women to indeterminate positions.

· · · · ·

Everyday I have some sense that it is somehow more difficult or there's more discrimination for women. I really believe that it exists and it exists in a pervasive way. I think it's deeply rooted in the corporate culture of government and in this department. For example, a few weeks ago my ADM made deprecating comments about two women with whom he was having debates on policy matters. When he talked about these women he dealt with them as personality problems. That's discrimination.

· · · · ·

Not everybody can be slapped on the face repeatedly and still keep coming back for more.

When you have ten men and one woman, a lot of men hiring don't want the woman because they're afraid that they're not going to be perceived as one of the boys.

· · · · ·

I've heard women say that they were appointed deputy minister because the men who made the decision needed women's names at the top, and put them in departments where they couldn't do too much damage when they failed. These male decision-makers are always surprised when women succeed as managers. When really important issues have to be settled, it's men's work.

· · · · ·

The idea is not that women should network among themselves, but rather that women have to build networks which include men, because the world we live and move in is still a male world. So most of my networks are not female. Because of my personal commitment and my own interests, I maintain contact with women at my own level, and try to keep track of what's happening to women in the public service and in business. But that is not the way I get decisions made. My decisions are made largely through my male networks. It's really unusual for a woman friend to be in my professional network where she and I make decisions, because the power structure is still largely male.

· · · · ·

I think women are far more flexible and democratic than men. We tend to measure output rather than whether you checked in at 8:00 and left at 5:00. As a manager I hope that I do this as much as I can. I don't watch the clock, but I do measure output. If I want a report by a certain time, I want the report. It doesn't matter if the employee leaves early and works at home, as long as I get the report. But I'm not sure men are ready for that. I think men are afraid that we might break down the structure of things.

· · · · ·

Historically rules and regulations were designed, composed and written by men. Never did they think that there might be a different viewpoint, another side of things. Women bring something very different, culturally very different, as we should. There's no humanity in the way things are now; rules and regulations have to have a human component.

· · · · ·

How does a woman operate in this system? Does the system have to be changed? It probably can't be changed. Therefore, a great deal of thought has to be given as to how the woman is prepared for this,

I think men are afraid that we might break down the structure of things.

because I don't think that women think in the same way as men. If she does think in the same way, she tends to become a little too masculine in her approach. This is why you really must have women in positions of responsibility in the public service. They are there not only because of their knowledge, but because of the way they deal with people and deal with problems. And you don't want to kill that by turning them into little artificial men.

· · · · ·

Of course my view of the world and that of my male colleagues is different, as it should be. I mean, that's why we all complement each other. It's so rich to have diverse views, regardless of language, race, origin, gender, whatever. I don't believe that this has been nurtured in the public service. The dominant model has been a military one which has been very successful! It's male. Very hierarchical. And paternalistic in the sense, "If you do what you're told I will look after you." Women work much better in a collegial atmosphere, teamwork. I think men have difficulty working in that model.

· · · · ·

Getting women into tough jobs is like turning the Queen Mary around on a pin.

Getting women into tough jobs is like turning the Queen Mary around on a pin. It takes a while to get it to budge, but once it starts to move, there is no stopping it.

· · · · ·

I recognize that there are women in lower-level positions than they should be. I attribute this to the attitude, on the part of some men (and men still make most of the choices) that they just would rather work with a man. I believe that some men still have difficulty dealing with women in the workplace. I know of one woman who was not recognized by her department (she "hit the glass ceiling"). Her reaction was to leave the public service. The department is only now waking up to the fact that a major female role model is leaving.

· · · · ·

They just don't understand the pain of being harassed or of trying to survive in their system.

· · · · ·

I wish one of the men in my workplace could be in my position as a woman for one week so that he could see how it feels. I've been totally excluded from the social aspects of my office because I am the only female professional. I've seen men being recognized and promoted over me and I've had my professional judgement questioned on a matter which I felt well qualified to deal with.

· · · · ·

I do not believe that the section to which I belong is aware of this situation (bias towards women) in a conscious sense, but the subliminal message is a powerful one. Because it is so ingrained and so undefined, it is a very difficult situation to be aware of, let alone fight against. I could not accuse the section of being malicious in its intent for I do not believe that to be the case. Rather, it is just following the usual power structure....of there being greater rewards for men than for women. For the most part, I think that the women who work here are glad to be on the playing field and have not yet begun to question whether the game is so heavily weighted that there is little hope of us ever being on the winning team.

(2) MILITARY/RCMP/CSIS INFLUENCE

The military create a closed shop for advancement from the writing of the job description right through the hiring process.

· · · · ·

There is a mind-set of ex-military officers (caused because) very few wives of military personnel are able to establish careers of their own. In addition, almost all of the colleagues and superiors of military men are other men. These two create a pattern that prevents them from seeing women as equals in the business world.

· · · · ·

Middle-level management is just chock-full of ex-military — it's like a solid wall mentality that anyone who is not military can't get through. If I had trouble with these guys, I imagine that a lot of women have difficulty breaking past this private gentlemen's club. I know how to get along with military guys. I've worked with them and they are people too, nice people, but do they deserve that extra advantage of the second career of being parachuted into jobs they really don't know? They're not good public servants, they are just good bureaucrats.

· · · · ·

... managers seem to see nothing wrong with bringing in retirees from DND who completed their technical training over 20 years ago and haven't really used it much for the past ten years. These newcomers are brought in as PG-4s with no knowledge of procurement. They are assigned Purchasing Assistants who are expected to teach these men all they need to know so they can qualify for PG-5 positions.

· · · · ·

I imagine that a lot of women have difficulty breaking past this private gentlemen's club.

The RCMP view women as wives and mothers. (She has been told her) work "is something to do until you marry and have children." There is a belief that women do clerical work because they enjoy it and are good at it.

・ ・ ・ ・ ・

Anytime a position has any responsibility or is anything more than "run-of-the-mill" it is held by a regular member of the RCMP... This applies to positions that do not require policing experience. This takes away opportunities for advancement, and the member transferred into the position is trained by a female public servant being paid half his wages.

・ ・ ・ ・ ・

They're not good public servants, they are just good bureaucrats.

The RCMP appear to believe that public servants have jobs, not careers; because we are women, the jobs are secondary income and therefore not of great consequence. This was again brought home to me recently when I was reminded that I was, after all, just a clerk.

・ ・ ・ ・ ・

When I ask my boss for lunch his expression is "What's wrong, do you wanna talk about it right now?" Then he sits on the edge waiting for the shoe to fall. "There's really nothing you want to talk about?" "No, just lunch." They're still not comfortable and it's hard to blame them, I mean it's the type of environment they came out of, military; they're more comfortable with the "boys."

・ ・ ・ ・ ・

When I went to Citizenship and Immigration I had a very difficult deputy. He was a typical military man. If it wasn't in the book he didn't do it. We wasted a lot of time arguing, which annoyed me.

・ ・ ・ ・ ・

It seems to me that until the structural underpinning of the federal civil service, involving such authoritarian, often centralized decision-making is changed, there is little room, nor advantage, for women to progress in the federal civil service.

(3) SEXIST LANGUAGE
The Treasury Board and the Public Service Alliance are still negotiating contracts in which all employees are automatically referred to as "he," the only exception being when the employee is being described as pregnant. The legal profession seems to have a lot of trouble admitting that two sexes exist when writing legal documents. Acts of Parliament are a case in point.

(4) DOUBLE STANDARD

(For a woman) assertiveness translates to "interpersonal problems" on appraisals: a man becomes a high flyer with a meteoric career.

· · · · ·

A woman who works in personnel came to me very upset. She said that she had been sitting in on employee appraisals and she noticed that every time they came to a woman they said that the woman was either too docile or too aggressive. She said that she had seen some of these women work and they are tremendously smart, there's nothing wrong with them. But, this is how they were rating these women all throughout the appraisals.

· · · · ·

Because my husband is a lawyer, I have been asked why I am holding down a job that belongs to someone else. No one asks men what their wives do for a living.

· · · · ·

I think women are discouraged from selling themselves. You know we hear about the aggressive woman, the bitchy woman, the forward woman, the castrating woman, etc., so women are socialized not to be that way. You tend to take a lot of this unwarranted criticism to heart. There is an enormous double standard when it comes to how men and women are judged. Women are judged much more harshly.

· · · · ·

Women should be considered as poor performers if they are not competent, not as a symbol that all women are unready to seek the heights.

· · · · ·

I don't really see why education should make more of a difference to women than to men.

· · · · ·

So I came into the labour shop. We had two older gentlemen here. They thought that women should be barefoot and pregnant and in the kitchen. No matter what I did, it was never good enough. It was all right if the men didn't do half the job, but they had to complain about somebody, and it was me. Women are always noticed. I didn't really care. I just did my work, and people knew that I was doing my work. My boss knew that I could always be found on the spot so he never said anything, but the older fellows kept an eye out to see where I was.

· · · · ·

If you show what you know you get branded pushy, aggressive, "Oh, another member of the National Advisory Council on the Status of Women on the loose" — that kind of thing.

· · · · ·

When I am interviewing for functional management or line management jobs what comes across most often is that we think of management as administrative implementation and if a woman thinks that way she is perceived as having a lack of leadership skills. If a man thinks that way, but uses a few leadership words throughout his interview, chances are he will be considered trainable. But because we still aren't used to thinking of women as leaders they are not inclined to be generous if a woman isn't aggressively a leader.

• • • • •

Most of the barriers I have encountered have related to individual managerial attitudes and lack of long-range planning rather than systemic barriers. In many ways these are the hardest barriers to overcome because they are niggardly and petty; thus, if one speaks out against them, one is considered thin-skinned or overly sensitive. I wish it were simpler to eradicate these attitudinal barriers; for many of them and for the individuals involved, training is just not enough. The underlying cultural perception of women in the work force as either not as competent as their male counterparts or as overly aggressive will not disappear in even one or two generations.

• • • • •

When a man gets posted overseas, they think about the woman's job, but they really don't work very hard at it. Whereas if a woman gets posted abroad, they're going to find a job for that guy, her husband. You know, this is quite frequent.

• • • • •

In our branch we've noticed that men are hesitant to move and sometimes they refuse to be transferred, but when there's a woman who is married the possibility of a transfer isn't even considered. Things are evolving though. They're starting to realize that you let people make their own decisions.

• • • • •

A lot of times I find that being a woman in the warehouse and in the position I have I would be able to get to the root of a personal problem that was getting in the way of work performance. There doesn't seem to be as much shame in telling a woman that you have a problem at home, so that helped once they got over the fact that I was female and more or less one of the boys, and that I didn't get all excited if they told me a dirty joke or swore.

• • • • •

If men are competitive it is a plus; if women are competitive it is considered a negative trait. It is hard to get it right.

• • • • •

If men are competitive it is a plus; if women are competitive it is considered a negative trait. It is hard to get it right.

Women have difficulty in management style. If they use an aggressive approach, they are "bitches." If they use a softer approach they are "weak." Each approach is seen positively in a man, either as results-oriented or consultative.

(5) NARROW BAND OF ACCEPTANCE
You have to make sure that you behave in an acceptable manner by a man's standards. We are still in a male-dominated era. In the traditional female roles there is a different behaviour.

. . . . .

You have to be ambitious but you cannot be too overt about it. You cannot be seen to be ambitious.

. . . . .

Once when I was turned down for a job I went to the director general and asked him why. He said that he had heard all kinds of good things about me, but he didn't like the way I looked. He said, "You know, I really have to be very honest" and I loved him for that — I mean I hated him for his decision, but he was honest with me. He said, "Your blonde hair, your looks — I was just scared away. I don't think that the package is there."

. . . . .

I have had male colleagues who have treated me with disdain because I am a woman. Some of the senior employees have been around here for a long time and they just don't want women around. There is some ugliness. For example, I was accused of going to bed with my boss. I had a lot in common with my boss and we would go for walks and out for lunch and this was misconstrued into an affair. We discussed how to handle this situation and I finally decided that I would not change my behaviour.

. . . . .

A narrow band of acceptable behaviour exists for women in senior positions. Women are not clear what is expected of them in such jobs; how to integrate themselves. Such women are expected to be not too feminine, but not too aggressive.

. . . . .

A lot of the barriers I have observed are attitudinal. Some of them are defences and habitual: a lot of them are subconscious. I have observed that you can talk to some of the older men in the system about their daughters, but if you talk about women's issues in abstract terms then they won't understand you.

(6) BATTERING

Our intelligence is insulted by management and our negative experiences laughed at or ridiculed by the men who work in the branch.

• • • • •

I have received comments such as "Why should I listen to you? You aren't an engineer. You're just a stupid woman."

• • • • •

The discrimination I experienced in my first year in Ottawa in the Canadian foreign service was manageable.... things like having a male manager tell me to get my hair cut.... From time to time I was asked if I was gay or otherwise hated men.

• • • • •

The day following the death of my father, the only remark that this supervisor made was that he supposed that we wouldn't get our marketing plan in on time since I would have to leave to attend my father's funeral.

• • • • •

One of the instructors used to stand up and tell penis envy jokes the first thing every morning. And some of my colleagues in the course were absolutely appalled. And I mean, I have a good sense of humor, but that is just a put down.

• • • • •

Three weeks after my supervisor's arrival, when I was working overtime on a Saturday morning, he entered my office and told me that personnel had warned him about me. I asked him what that meant and he said he had simply been warned.

• • • • •

There was a case where a woman went through legal channels to right a wrong! and won! But what it did to her mentally, you can't describe it. She got to the point where she herself doubted her own capability. She had to take a demotion and take a job somewhere else. She's happy now, but imagine having to go through that.

• • • • •

I am a journeyman landscape gardener, have an associate diploma in horticulture from university and 14 years of experience. When I was in the process of divorcing my husband and very unsure of my future, my boss used to remark that if he was my husband he would "Beat me black and blue." He blamed me constantly, in front of others, every day, for things he knew I had no control over. He said that I would be too weak for the hard work, that women just wanted a man's wage for doing half the work. I grieved this personal harassment and got letters

Why should I listen to you? You aren't an engineer. You're just a stupid woman.

of support and witnesses to his behaviour. I did win, at second level ...
but even then it was because of his known habit of drinking on the job
and his bad management record. All the people I talked to (except the
union) minimized his habits. They intimated that it was my fault ...
that perhaps he was joking.

After he received a letter of reprimand, he tried to transfer me, as he
had threatened, as punishment. He was upheld in this by two levels
of management as his "Right to manage," before the assistant
supervisor (a woman) put a stop to it.

This summer, he has either left me alone or treated me with respect,
but I feel that as retribution, he and management have decided never
to promote me. When I asked why I was not considered for an acting
position, everyone looked surprised and murmured something about
"Personality conflict."... It seems obvious that my boss abuses his position ... but he is allowed to do these things because it is O.K. by his
superiors. Women should be given more than just words when it
comes to men like this.

· · · · ·

At one time I got access to my file. It was quite devastating to go
through it. I discovered things like instructions telling certain people
that they shouldn't be afraid of me. There was also a comment that
said that at the end of my term they should offer me a position that I
would not accept. In other words, they played games with me.

· · · · ·

Those people who either hated me because I was female or were
threatened because I was going to make changes acted in a variety of
ways. I mean they sent brown paper envelopes to MPs, they tried to
arouse scandals, they tried to destroy me.

· · · · ·

Once we were having a meeting in my office, with lawyers from the
department. I was expressing my opinion about an issue, when I
turned around and saw this lawyer making fun of me, ridiculing me,
behind my back. I just glared at him and he knew that I saw him making signs to the effect that I was a little crazy. That's a terrible situation,
to have a staff member making jokes behind your back.

· · · · ·

I think that sexual harassment is easier to deal with than what I call
mental harassment. If your boss has a wrong idea about you, you don't
know what he is thinking because he is not conscious of the fact that
he has judged you. You know sexual harassment when it happens, it is

unmistakable behaviour and you can let him have it there and then. But this other thing, how do you deal with it?

· · · · ·

I talked to a secretary about her boss. She is a good secretary, but he refuses to get organized or let her organize him, and loses things and claims he never had them. She finally questioned her own ability, unsure if she had actually taken stuff in to him; her ego had been slowly eaten away. I think that is much more worrisome, and I see far too much of it. They can't get at you in obvious ways because of the human rights laws and merit review, but they can certainly make you feel worthless.

(7) HARASSMENT

When I first started working as a clerk, I was the only female in that office. I believed that the looks, comments, treatment were what every woman had to put up with. I would blush, ignore and avoid certain co-workers. I was told that the woman in the position before me quit in the middle of the day, crying. The comments were that she had no sense of humor.

· · · · ·

The harasser is doing quite well... All of us are considered as problems, not the harasser.

My superior would ask me out at least once a week. As my tolerance level became thin, I made my position clearer, but "NO" was not the response he expected. His affection soon turned to personal harassment, although he stated I knew exactly how things could be better. After several years, I was no longer alone, so several of us put in a complaint to the PSC. It is two years later and our complaint is still not settled. The harasser is doing quite well — supervising and acting in the manager's position. I moved (a five-hour drive from my husband and children). Others involved have resigned, transferred or remained there in frustration. All of us are considered as problems, not the harasser.

· · · · ·

The real problem is not that one man exists who upsets so many women, but that all of us went quietly to management and to personnel, but all of us were hushed, or told something would be done, or told we were trying to cause trouble in a nice office environment.

· · · · ·

(While travelling, my boss) dragged me around, showed me off and tried to imply that we were sleeping together.... He created work to ensure that I could not see other friends while travelling, and generally treated me as his property.

· · · · ·

I was harassed by one gentleman so much that I had to go see his manager (also mine) and tell him that unless he did something about the situation, I would have to file a grievance. They talked to him, made him apologize to me, but I am the one who received a poor evaluation and was told that I don't interact well with others and have a bad attitude. The gentleman in question received a glowing evaluation.

. . . . .

Management allows the harassment (of whole sections) to continue.

. . . . .

Julie was sexually harassed by one of her colleagues. She asked her supervisor for assistance. In an extremely embarrassed fashion, he advised her that she would have to face up to the situation alone and let her know that he would close his eyes if she resorted to violence to defend herself. After a particularly intolerable incident, to which there were witnesses, she confronted the individual. This was very difficult for her, especially because he started to cry. However, he did apologize and the harassment stopped.

. . . . .

Women in senior levels are more likely to insist that something be done about sexual harassment. Harassers continue to get away with it, though; either it's covered up or the woman is convinced to quit bugging the managers, or they move her someplace. In too many cases, the guy keeps working and the woman loses her job.

. . . . .

My signed metal Frederickson framing square had been twisted into a (gnarled) knot, dumped on my desk and "CUNT" had been written in big letters on my desk.

. . . . .

After three years of studying without coming across any (attitude) problems I walked into the fourth-year classroom and on the back wall, I mean we are talking 1981 and I expected more than that, were three "crotch-shot" poster-sized pictures of women. I went to the back to the wall and took the pictures down because by then I had learned that I had something to teach those guys.

. . . . .

I spent six months in probably the worst hell of my life while studying with 15 young men, 18 to 24 most of them, who had all gone north to prove their manhood by trying to get rid of the women who were in the class. I was the first woman to go through any trades training at that school and I was told constantly about the one that didn't make it. Everyday there would be tits on the blackboard, signs on the tool room door or other stuff.

. . . . .

SECTION 3
The System

(1) STAFFING SYSTEMS

(A) Management Resource Information System

MRIS is supposed to be a vehicle for identifying candidates. As we are never aware that we have been pulled off MRIS and rejected, we have no means to reverse the decision and put forward our particular qualities related to the job in question.

· · · · ·

For the past three years I have been seconded to the Department of External Affairs as an FS-2 (SM minus 1 level) from my position at another department as an ES-4 (SM minus 3 level).... Judging that my next logical career move would be to the SM level, I approached the PSC and asked to be included in the MRIS. Since my substantive level is ES-4, this has been denied. An individual cannot be denied the right to enter a public service competition on the basis of salary; however, that right can be denied on the basis of level and classification, which are closely tied to salary.

· · · · ·

A major obstacle to advancement in the PS is the combination of recruitment, personnel practices and job posting procedures. MRIS doesn't work. My name hasn't come up once in seven years. Either I am not useful to anyone or the system doesn't work. I prefer the latter interpretation. Jobs are posted on a clipboard located in the corridor of the personnel office. There is no privacy, nor can you peruse the posting at your leisure. Also, they are late. Thus it is not easy to become aware of job opportunities or to take advantage of them. The provincial government publishes a newspaper called "Job Mart" which posts all job openings weekly and is distributed to the desks of all employees.

The kind of discrimination which concerns me is ... the invisibility of women in the informal selection process.

(B) The Informal System Excludes Women

The kind of discrimination which concerns me is ... the invisibility of women in the informal selection process which identifies officers with potential and grooms them for the future.

• • • • •

If a woman's qualifications are not quite right, she is likely to be screened out. They don't screen out the men, but they do screen out the women.

• • • • •

I have very often heard people say that it was the male on their team to whom the developmental and training opportunities were given. In one case a young man was given all the interesting assignments and developmental opportunities despite the fact that there was a woman who had been there for years, knew the place inside and out and was very capable. I have no trouble believing that this is a very widespread phenomenon. Any training I've received has been on my own instigation.

• • • • •

A good number of my male colleagues have in fact been given active boosts to their careers by being staffed by personnel into high-profile jobs, often as underfills, and working for high-profile supervisors. Not surprisingly, they have done considerably better in terms of appraisals and promotions, not just because they are able officers but because they have been given the training and monitoring to make them even more effective.

• • • • •

... if you wanted to move and be a high flyer, either the Treasury Board or Finance was it and ... if you look at Stats Canada you see a lot of women, not right at the top but a lot of women statisticians and economists, highly qualified. So there wasn't a shortage, there were not a lot of qualified women but it wasn't as though they didn't exist. How come none of them were in the two elite departments?

• • • • •

... when push came to shove and it was a question of an appointment on merit, and I have to stress that point, in my view if I had been male I would have been without question in one of the two top positions for a career strength of a person who is highly trained in a technical area. So I followed the exit strategy.

• • • • •

If I had been male I would have been in one of the two top positions...So I followed the exit strategy.

Many women officers have also found that male supervisors are less likely to give women challenging assignments or job packages with major responsibilities, making it less easy for them to demonstrate their effectiveness and potential.

* * * * *

When I was in management processing I had been doing a lot of work back and forth in Washington because we were going to use their computers. I had a lot of experience and I really knew more about it than anybody. The director of the division called me and said that they really wanted a hotshot to go down to Washington for six weeks to learn all about it. Neither one of the men he was considering knew as much as I did. What could I say? So, one of these guys got the trip to Washington. They did not even consider me for this even though I was doing it all. At the end of this six-week term he decided to go back to school, so all that experience was lost.

* * * * *

They did not even consider me even though I was doing it all.

I have listed below in point form several situations which arose for me which prevented my advancement in the federal public service and which eventually forced me to leave:

- I applied for a PM-5 position, the next highest level to the one I was in, and was told that I did not have the managerial experience to qualify for it.
- I asked my supervisor to designate me to act in his position (PM-5) when he took his annual month-long vacation, to allow me to gain managerial experience. He was never prepared to do so.
- Aware that I must be bilingual to do most management jobs, on my own time I took three years of evening classes sponsored by the PSC.... after achieving a C level in both the written and comprehension areas, I asked for intensive training in oral French and was denied this.
- In the hope that I would have better access to advancement in a larger centre, I approached the PSC to assist me in arranging a transfer to Edmonton. I was able to get minimal assistance only, as I did not live in Alberta and was not considered a priority transfer.
- When the same position that I was doing in Saskatchewan opened up in Edmonton the PSC and departmental management allowed the manager to hold an open competition for the position instead of transferring me, and to change the qualifications and description of the position in mid-competition, to have CCC French requirements so that I was excluded.

(C) Selection Process Discriminates Against Women with Children

(The manager told me that) a woman told the selection board that her child's health came before her work, so her application was dismissed.

· · · · ·

I was a member of a selection board and the other members were asking dumb questions such as "What are your intentions about family?" and so on. I was so annoyed at a member of a selection committee who asked a woman this. The next candidate was a man so I asked him "What about your family? How many children have you got? What are your intentions about enlarging it? Is it going to interfere with your work?"... he was so discomforted and so were the others on the board ... but how else do you make the point?

(D) General

Right now the Public Service Commission controls everything from promotions to personnel functions. It has rules for everything from competition to positions to classification. Departments are at the mercy of the Public Service Commission. The Commission is really too big and it's trying to do too much. When the Commission realizes it's having a bad effect on an area, it puts in more regulations, which confuses everyone. I think this is one barrier, because to accomplish anything, you have to go around the rules.

· · · · ·

The biggest barrier I experienced was the *Public Service Employment Act*. It started out as something genuine, but now it's just one regulation on top of another.

· · · · ·

What does the PSC do? They're so bogged down in rules and forms and bureaucracy that they don't have time to think about people.

· · · · ·

I requested an interview with the Bank of Canada with the head of the research department and I was given a long leisurely interview and discussed my thesis and work I had published and the rest of it, and when I had got up, he said "I'll be back in touch with you". It is now (30 years later) and I have never heard.

· · · · ·

I realized I was going to be part of the top echelons of the public service. I was a trained economist. I spent a long time maintaining my credentials. ...I continued to publish. I continued to read, I did everything I could ... to keep my capacity going....In a system based on merit which I had believed this was, I would end up at a logical destination. I was proven wrong.

• • • • •

The rigidity of the staffing system makes it difficult (but not impossible) to select high potential individuals who do not yet demonstrate the skills needed.

• • • • •

If you know someone it really helps. Most competitions are cooked — it's so easy to do it. Given two individuals with the same qualifications, the individual with connections gets the job.

• • • • •

There is too much emphasis on the board interview in the selection process. People who don't interview well are not selected, even though they may be very well qualified to do the job. More emphasis should be placed on the candidate's track record and appraisals.

• • • • •

What helps to advance? You have to be a good actor, a person who can cram for an interview and sell yourself. The board process is a ridiculous process — they do not even consider previous managers' reviews.

• • • • •

In the public service staffing process, potential does not count for much. The way in which the merit principle is interpreted in most departments is you have to have done the job before you can get it.

• • • • •

The competition process isn't fair. There are no standards across groups, people are parachuted into positions. People still get jobs because they know someone. All this causes resentment.

• • • • •

It's a hell of a lot easier in the public sector. In the public sector ordinary women make it. In the private sector only women who are extraordinary in work, looks and/or connections make it.

• • • • •

The federal government practice of posting job competitions is a major barrier in the region when looking for a job. Because I am on secondment, the problem is magnified as I'm unable to walk by the bulletin board located in the personnel department without a special trip. It's only by luck that I find out about openings. Thus, contacts are extremely important; but it would be nice to have a formal communication system that worked better.

• • • • •

In the public service staffing process, potential does not count for much. You have to have done the job before you can get it.

There is a strong need to reduce the rigidity of the staffing process. There is too much stress on competitions as the prime mode of career advancement. The public service has been caught in a "merit" trap. Instead, the public service needs a blend of competitive processes and more creative assignments and developmental processes.

· · · · ·

It is important to develop selection techniques which do not arbitrarily rule out women. The in-basket exercise would be a good example of such a technique.

· · · · ·

The public service needs to recruit new people desperately. There is too much deadwood; we need new ideas. We need to recruit from labour, academe, the private sector.

· · · · ·

One big problem is recruitment. We're missing a whole generation. We need fresh talent, enthusiasm, new perspectives. We should be recruiting recent graduates into the support category, mentoring them, sending employees on educational leave, pressuring people to retire.

(2) UNJUSTIFIED EDUCATIONAL BARRIERS

I was a CO-1, acting in a CO-2 position and being appraised as Fully Satisfactory as a CO-2 at every appraisal period. According to my manager, I could not be appointed as a CO-2 because I did not have a degree — it did not matter what degree I had, as long as I had that little piece of paper.

· · · · ·

Fewer and fewer positions are available to me due to the high percentage of positions requiring a degree with no allowance being made for equivalency gained by on-the-job experience.... I recently applied for a PM-6 position with Status of Women Canada for which I believed I was well qualified only to once again be screened due to the fact that I lack the education requirements. It is very disappointing to find that this department in particular also supports the "No Equivalency" practice.

· · · · ·

Education does not always replace experience.... For many competitions, educational requirements are much too high. For example, on a recent AS-1 poster, a university or college education was required.

· · · · ·

The District Director is a graduate of vocational school. A Clerk in the regional office has successfully graduated from the same school with excellent marks. She has, in addition to the vocational school certificate, nearly one full year of the two-year technical institute course, several years of experience with the department and some evening technical courses. The department refuses to allow the Clerk to apply for an EL-1 trainee position. They claim her years with the department do not count as the 80 hours of experience needed to make up the difference between vocational and technical school. The department first told the Clerk she could not be accepted because the union would object to this "lowering" of the standards. The IBEW stated that they had no objection. The department then claimed that the PSC would not accept the Clerk for a referral. When the PSC accepted her qualifications and referred her for an interview, the department flatly refused to accept her: she was screened out and not allowed to compete.

She was originally employed as a CR-4, then had to quit to attend school full-time. She is now a CR-3, better educated but worse off than when she started pursuing her goal to better herself.

The District Director (EL-7) has fewer academic qualifications than the Clerk. Do you really need higher qualifications to be an EL-1 than you do to be an EL-7? Or do you only need them if you are female?

* * * * *

I would say the biggest barrier in the federal government has been my lack of a university degree. There have been many occasions when opportunities could have been there if I had that piece of paper.

* * * * *

It is essential to create the proper environment in the public service to encourage women's advancement. For example, many selection standards require educational qualifications which are not really needed.

* * * * *

Specialized educational or experience requirements can effectively screen women out of competitions. It becomes a convenient excuse that "no qualified women are available." There are a variety of recruitment and development techniques which can be used, including: formal training and development programs, bridging positions and university recruitment.

* * * * *

When post-secondary education is stated as a requirement for a position, perhaps allow those without this formal education but with work experience to take an exam in lieu. This would allow these employees to get a foot in the door.

* * * * *

Education is definitely a facilitator. On the other hand it is an artificial one for women. In effect women's experience is undervalued. Thus, women have to acquire additional credentials to be certain they meet the grade.

• • • • •

Degrees are seen as more important than work-related experience. It is therefore often difficult for secretaries to meet the typical education requirements of positions which they are otherwise qualified for.

• • • • •

Having worked on both sides of the fence (public and private sectors) I've noted that as an employee in the federal government one is exposed to a much greater range of clients. The government corporate culture is similar to that of a large corporation. The advantage of the corporate sector is that employees are rewarded for merit, and not qualifications, for example, university degrees.

(3) BRIDGING PROGRAMS

I don't think I would ever have gotten here based on today's standards for bridging the gap — there aren't the administrative trainee programs any more, there aren't many ways of bridging that gap.

• • • • •

Everything I have seen for special advantages for women in the work force has been offered to those in the SM or SM-1 categories. If you are fortunate enough to have a university degree you have a great opportunity to be in those pay categories and take advantage of these opportunities. I am all for it. What about the rest of us — the vast majority of female staff in the lower clerical and secretarial levels? What about encouraging "advancement from within"? What about programs to provide women with the opportunity to advance to the low and middle management levels? Why does everything appear to be for senior levels?

• • • • •

I joined External Affairs as a SCY-1 in 1981, with an Honours B.A. and two years teaching experience in Nigeria. I worked as a secretary for four years at the Canadian Embassy in Bangkok. On my return to Canada I consulted with my personnel officer about career advancement opportunities, producing my last appraisal (rated as Outstanding) and references from my various supervisors.... she informed me that there were no avenues by which secretaries could switch to PM positions. I took education leave to pursue a scholarship program to a Master's degree in Public Administration. When I was due to graduate,

What about encouraging "advancement from within"?

I was again advised that there were no opportunities. I then resigned from the federal public service until I was able to enter the foreign service from the outside six months later.

· · · · ·

Even when alleged developmental opportunities are offered they tend to be laterals in disguise. Our secretary, who wants to get into the audit field, was offered a developmental secondment at the AS-1 level by Treasury Board. First, the pay was changed to continue at her SCY-3 rate and then, as the secondment developed, she discovered more and more that all the receiving department wanted was a free secretary. My conclusion from this and other observations is that most secondments relating to women are, at best, laterals in disguise, and do absolutely nothing to create developmental opportunities.

(4) INADEQUATE CAREER AND GUIDANCE COUNSELLING

The situation (with respect to women in non-traditional trades) will not change drastically until women/girls are shown in their formative years, that there are other opportunities out there in the work force than nurse, teacher, secretary, etc.

· · · · ·

(At Transport Canada) the emphasis is on outside recruitment. (This is not surprising) given that there is little apparent human resource or career path planning.

· · · · ·

When I first moved to headquarters here, I was told that there would be a career plan made up for me; I've never seen it.

· · · · ·

There have been some very great women who have been here and have left because there has been little career development.

· · · · ·

Career planning and career development are mysteries that only personnel understands.

· · · · ·

Lack of career paths is a real problem. There is a lack of sponsors/mentors/counsellors; there is nobody who says "you should do this next if you want to go for that." You're on your own 100%!

· · · · ·

One barrier is the complete lack of career counselling. This is particularly noticeable in a department which is responsible for employment equity and for counselling workers.

· · · · ·

Even when alleged developmental opportunities are offered they tend to be laterals in disguise.

My name was submitted to the PSC as a woman who should be groomed for a managerial position. I went to see someone and they said: "At your level you can't go anywhere. You're too low. We only talk to people at one level below SM. So when you get there, call us back."

• • • • •

There is no point in having career counselling services if they are not effective. All it does is get people's hopes up then it knocks them down — and the frustration continues.

• • • • •

A major barrier is the lack of career planning at the individual level and human resource planning at a more macro level. Every move I made was on my own. No one opens any doors in the public service.

• • • • •

There are no clear career paths defined by the Public Service Commission; there is no career counselling available formally in the public service. Career paths are decided by individuals with occasional help from their managers.

• • • • •

Make sure that the Counselling Bureau for women keeps up or even doubles its effort so when a manager is ready to staff a position he could be reminded that there are lists of women.

• • • • •

It is essential that there be a real career plan for talented women from the time they enter the federal public service. Also they should be encouraged not to linger too long in the same position.

(5) APPRAISAL

I heard from someone who works in personnel that for quite a few years I had been identified as a "high flyer." I am in this book, but I have never heard about it, and was turned down to go on CAP.

• • • • •

In the Department of External Affairs, if one does not receive a consistent Superior or Outstanding appraisal, the opportunity to advance is all but absent. I received a less than complimentary appraisal. It arrived seven months after the assignment had been completed. I attempted on six or seven occasions to meet with my supervisor.... he simply didn't show up.

• • • • •

Reports which contain comments like, "she has a bubbly and effervescent personality," which tell you nothing about the professional qualities of the woman, should be sent back for rewriting.

• • • • •

Career planning and career development are mysteries that only personnel understands.

... valid certified leave, taken to nurse a sick child, was remarked on detrimentally in my appraisal.

．　．　．　．　．

One barrier to women in the public service is the absence of a good, realistic appraisal process. The present appraisal process is wishy-washy. It does not provide valuable realistic feedback. The performance appraisal system must be improved. The system is there but the application is lacking. It is not a useful tool as it now stands. Everyone is Fully Satisfactory. Results are taken with a grain of salt by managers in regards to promotion. They are "beige," saying nothing substantive.

．　．　．　．　．

At present, performance appraisals are a joke. My boss is four levels higher than me and doesn't know how to appraise me. He does not understand my work.

．　．　．　．　．

The appraisal system supposedly identifies superior performers (high flyers) but appraisals do not seem to have much impact in staffing.

．　．　．　．　．

The performance appraisal system can be very frustrating. If an employee disagrees with something, the only recourse is not to sign and be branded as a troublemaker.

．　．　．　．　．

There wasn't any sense of reward. You get a good evaluation, but then it's never confirmed by the way you're treated.

．　．　．　．　．

Recognition and rewards go together. A major problem is that there are no rewards for work well done. As a manager, you have to break the rules to reward your own staff, like allowing them a day off. You also spend your own money on rewards for them. There are quotas for Superior ratings so all the people deserving them do not get them. In my case, my own boss does say thank you and does give me feedback, but this is unusual. There are not many good managers in the public service. Very few say thank you or recognize good work.

．　．　．　．　．

There are problems with the reward system. It is not flexible enough. With a merit system that is rigid and exclusionary, many managers with excellent appraisals do not get rewards. At the same time, managers have to pay for rewards for their staff, such as flowers or lunches, out of their own pockets.

．　．　．　．　．

Valid certified leave, taken to nurse a sick child, was remarked on detrimentally in my appraisal.

There is a lack of recognition for work well done. Senior managers take all the credit. It should be considered part of managers' jobs to give recognition when it is deserved. Recognition is the main reward, since a pay cheque is construed as a given.

(6) TRAINING

The training opportunities offered to women in the public service are limited and seem chiefly confined to making them better at their existing jobs — when what is really needed is to give them the marketable skills to break into other areas.

· · · · ·

What type of courses are available for ST-SCY-2s who want to advance, to expand their knowledge, to move into another occupational group with the same employer?

· · · · ·

When one public servant requested a detachment clerk course so she could move into that area from her CR-3 position, she was told that public servants are only given training required to do their present position as the RCMP was not in the habit of training employees for other jobs.

· · · · ·

Management does not approve courses taken by clerical workers unless they directly relate to their position. In my particular case I had signed up for a word processing course at the advanced level, having already completed the beginner level using my own money. Rather than consider a transfer to even the steno pool (where I could use this newly acquired skill, which is not what I really want to do; but perhaps I could work my way into supervising the pool, or working as an executive secretary for a section head) I was refused reimbursement costs as it did not relate to my position... A closed door to getting ahead... A prerogative set with tunnel vision.

· · · · ·

It's not normal for managers in government to send women on a lot of conferences. We should be sending them on these conferences, whether they're North American or international conferences. The same thing applies to training. Women don't seem to get enough training. Sending women on seminars will allow them to talk with people from other organizations.

· · · · ·

The RCMP was not in the habit of training employees for other jobs.

There is a sad lack of training funds available for women. The branch has a large training budget, but I'm sure that less than 10% is used to train women.... when the training plan is being prepared, management usually "writes in" a couple of courses which are usually of no interest to the employee.

· · · · ·

Training during the day was made available to 12 male counsellors. Support staff were told that if they took night courses they would be reimbursed. It is extremely difficult for a woman with young children to take courses two nights a week along with studying and the preparation of reports.

· · · · ·

One time we offered these training courses to women, in conjunction with Algonquin College. Men could go on these courses as well, but they were really for women. The men taking these courses could go home and do their homework. However, the women still had to look after the kids, cook dinner, etc., so they just did not have the time to do their homework. So, we had to give the women time at work to do their supplementary work for the course. That was the only way these women could stay in the course.

· · · · ·

On a recent PSC course. ... A video presentation showed the woman in a stereotypical manner. She was not ever shown teaching the skills, only learning from a man. She was twice the victim of a car breakdown, in which she called her male friend to correct a coil problem and to bring gas for her. Unfortunately, she was often shown as unable to handle the situations by herself, when he was always shown in a positive and confident manner and showing her where she had "gone wrong."

(7) CLASSIFICATION AND COMPENSATION

(A) Classification
The rigidity of the classification system is there for a number of reasons but there are very serious problems in overcoming that, in spotting talent.

· · · · ·

When I was a CR-4 and had 250 clerks I suddenly realized that here I was a CR-4 while there were people around me who were much higher and had fewer staff. So, I went to them and told them that I wasn't very happy about what was going on. I was told that they were redoing the CR category and that I would probably get a promotion after this was done. So I sat and waited and the new categories came out and sure enough I was still a CR-4. Then I went to see the director of personnel and told him that they were taking advantage of me and I wanted to quit. He told me to stay and they would get a CR-6 advertised right away. So the competition was advertised and of course I won because I had been doing the work all along. But if I had not said anything they would have continued to take advantage of me. I think organizations do that. It is easier to take advantage of people than to do what you should be doing. One lesson I learned was that if you don't scream they won't do anything.

One lesson I learned was that if you don't scream they won't do anything.

· · · · ·

(On moving from a secretary to an administrative assistant) To the woman it looks terrific — a move up out of the secretarial ranks, but in fact all they are doing is secretarial work and they are not acquiring any new skills.

· · · · ·

We are often required to supervise CR-4s who make as much money as we do and who are only required to have secondary school education.

· · · · ·

The classification and pay systems have gone berserk. You have a circumstance where various classifications are termed equivalents, but they are not equivalent in pay bands. I have had circumstances in which I could not hire someone from another department because we were out $130.00 on a pay band.

· · · · ·

I am now an Administrative Assistant — a position that is not recognized in the hierarchy of the federal government as a distinct occupation. I have been slotted in several different categories, depending on the service or the department, throughout the Government because "it doesn't fit anywhere." The job doesn't have any nice, neat job description....Because it is not "classifiable" by personnel standards... my classification has been in question and hashed over for the last six years, never with the same result. This is ludicrous. This is a job which women do well and the classification needs to be set to show the worth of the "jack-of-all-trades" skills required to fill it.

(B) Payback of Superannuation Benefits after Care and Nurturing Leave

The problem I had was that after a three-year leave of absence, whether I returned to work or not, I would have had to reimburse my pension benefits, which would have been about $900/month. If you quit you still have to reimburse them $1000. It's financially foolish. If it hadn't been for that pension I probably would have taken a three-year leave of absence, it would have been foolish not to. I looked at all the options available to me, but decided I had to quit.

(C) Allowable Child-care Expenses
The amounts for child care while mothers travel on business are inadequate and would not meet, for example, minimum pay requirements set out by Ontario legislation for domestic employees.

· · · · ·

When I was a senior manager I had to travel a lot. I was responsible for the liaison programs with all offices around the country. There is a Treasury Board directive that allows you to be reimbursed for the cost of babysitters if you are a single mother or your husband is physically unable to care for the children. My husband was physically able, but he had to travel a lot on business. It doesn't make sense. It became very costly to travel. I would have to spend $150 for three evenings away from home. The directive should have applied to everyone who has to travel.

(8) PART-TIME AND TERM EMPLOYMENT
My manager decided that because we were in a period of restraint, all women who were on part-time would have to go back to work full-time, or forget it. People who were on a compressed work week had to go back to a regular work week.

· · · · ·

I requested part-time work (after returning early from maternity leave) and it was denied by the ADM (who had become hostile since I had ignored his verbal sexual harassment.) My case was raised with the DM ... who directed that part-time work be available on a trial basis.

Part-time work was permitted for four months: during that time, I was sent on six business trips in the course of three months, compared to two half-day trips a year in the three years previous. Notwithstanding, I carried out all tasks agreed upon at the outset of the four-month trial.

Only one week after the commencement of the part-time work week, my manager told me that under no circumstances would the arrangement be continued after the four-month period. Last week was the end of the four-month trial. All goals were met, (despite having

It's financially foolish. I looked at all the options but decided I had to quit.

been expanded during the trial period), but the arrangement was terminated nevertheless.

• • • • •

It seems discriminatory (since the vast majority of part-time employees are women) that seasonal employees can contribute to superannuation based on time worked, while part-time employees cannot. Although I worked for three years as an indeterminate employee at three days per week, none of this is counted as pensionable time ... This situation has pushed the year at which I can retire from 2011 to 2013. While working part-time you are also not allowed to withdraw pension contributions made to date for re-investment in a private pension plan; your superannuation is basically frozen until you return to work full-time.

• • • • •

In one section where I worked, in a massive department, there were 29 term employees. They all went through tremendous stress every six months ... they had no means of knowing whether their terms would be extended or not.

(9) REORGANIZATION

In August 1986, a decision was made to amalgamate my branch with another. I had just negotiated a possible career development assignment, but my manager requested that I stay and help with the reorganization. When the dust settled from this shuffle, I requested a career development assignment and was accepted. Unfortunately, my manager was again heavily involved in a reorganization, this time an integration with another department. Again, he requested my assistance. ... loyalty, dedication and responsibility are not just buzz words to me. I take them very seriously. Also, the possibility of a supervisory role was suggested, so once again I put my plans aside. The past 1-1/2 years has been very difficult, but challenging. Many new duties, roles and responsibilities have been assigned to me — with no remuneration outside of my appraisal.

Job descriptions are being re-written and it now appears that my position will be downgraded to a SCY-2, where I was seven years ago.

• • • • •

... support staff have been reduced disproportionately to the officer and management staff. This has greatly increased the workload of the remaining support staff, and, as a by-product, means that officers often have to perform their own support duties.

... support staff have been reduced disproportionately to the officer and management staff.

(10) SPOUSAL RELOCATION
Requires going on a priority list i.e. you must stop work.

・・・・・

Because my spouse's promotion to Lieutenant-Colonel necessitated a temporary move to Halifax, I requested a lateral transfer to that area. To facilitate my request, my manager initiated an exchange between my office and the Halifax region. The proposed exchange was accepted by several layers of management and the region involved, but was refused by the Assistant Deputy Minister of Personnel. The reasons given were extremely arbitrary and based on technicalities.

(11) TARGETS AND QUOTAS
I have heard more statements that "ALL YOU NEED IS TO BE A WOMAN IN THIS TOWN OR IN THE GOVERNMENT AND YOU CAN WRITE YOUR OWN TICKET."

・・・・・

They (targets and quotas) seek to promote by exception rather than ability. As a woman, I hope to succeed by expertise and knowledge as opposed to sex. Being made an exception to the rule breeds tension and hostility ... you have to work harder and better to prove your worth while developing an unfair and undeserved reputation.

・・・・・

In 1981 I won a position through a national competition, I thought, not unreasonably ... because my experience was relevant and I had a good track record. A point made to me soon after my arrival and frequently in the course of my stay there, was that I was hired because the director was forced to meet an established quota of females.

In my third year ... I won a competition for a secondment but my director refused to give me permission to accept it, despite the fact that there was no loss of resources to him.... It is my speculation that he refused to do so so as not to jeopardize his ability to meet his quota of women.

I think if anything has impeded these special action groups, it's the quota system. I am dead set against it. Quotas also put a heavy burden on women. There are incompetent women as well as men. So if a woman moves into a position and fails, the senior manager who hired her says, "Well, I hired a woman once and she didn't work out." It kills any short-term opportunities for women. That's tragic and I think the quota system is causing that to happen to a certain degree.

・・・・・

> *A point made to me soon after my arrival was that I was hired to meet an established quota.*

I have always just bulled ahead and done what I had to do. So far, I have got pretty well what I want, most of the time. I always seem to be the token woman; people assume I have the job because I'm female. The more comfortable ones tell me that some people here feel they can't tell me technical things because I won't understand, so I have to prove that I can. A retiree told me, "You know, I've had to tell them down there that you're smarter than most of them."

· · · · ·

It's important not only to have women advancing, but also to ensure that employees and chiefs have the correct attitude towards women advancing. The quota system produces a "filling in the squares" mentality — "We've got one! Now we don't have to worry any more!" If you hire people for any reason other than ability, then why would you ever consider promoting them?

· · · · ·

I don't think that you need to set up special situations for women because they're women. That makes it more difficult for women to operate on the same plane.

· · · · ·

If you are in a senior position, you like to feel that you made it on your own merit, and it's a bit unpleasant when you feel that somebody could look at you and say "Oh well, a token woman."

· · · · ·

I was made acting chief, and after a year or so they rather wanted me to take it over on a permanent basis. Trying to persuade me, he said "Well, if it helps at all, we've decided to make it a full directorship and not just a chief." Then he said something that rather put me off: "We thought it would be rather nice to have the first woman director." I didn't feel quite right being a "token" woman.

· · · · ·

You think of the people who are now teaching your kids. If they're there because of a quota and they're not in fact the best people for the job that's scary. Just hiring me because I'm a woman is not going to make it for me.

· · · · ·

I think women have to be honest with themselves, as do employers. Don't hire me because I'm a woman because you're not doing me any bloody favour. It's difficult enough being in a job as a woman without being an incompetent woman because you sure as hell aren't going to survive.

· · · · ·

After I got the job at the EX level, my boss told me that he had had strict instructions that he must hire a woman for that job. So, he started asking people if they knew of any credible woman who could make things happen. He was very unhappy about being forced to hire a woman. However, after I had been there for about a month, he called me into his office and told me that he was very pleased with my work.

· · · · ·

They've just appointed a new ADM who is a Francophone female engineer. There's a lot of muttering going around about satisfying a lot of your quotas with one move!

· · · · ·

The general resentment caused by "affirmative action" programs and hiring quotas for women is undermining their original intent. When women are hired in current competitions, too often their competence is immediately questioned by those who feel that they were chosen for gender reasons alone. I feel that most women would rather compete on their own merits.

· · · · ·

I don't want to have to go to Equal Opportunities to get advancement. I know a lot of female air traffic controllers feel that way. Unfortunately as soon as you start getting ahead people think that that is why.

· · · · ·

Target groups are more likely to be given training for appearances sake; to meet quotas.

· · · · ·

Quotas and women on selection boards do not help. They introduce uncertainties into the process as to why women were selected for a position.

· · · · ·

Parachuting women into jobs which they cannot handle is damaging to all women.

· · · · ·

Quotas do not work. A systems solution will not work. Managers are very adept at side-stepping systems to get what they want. Somehow, managers must develop a commitment to change. A good manager can walk around the system, but one committed manager will do more than all the systems.

· · · · ·

Programs such as Equal Opportunity for Women, Affirmative Action, Employment Equity, are not the answer. They help women who work in them but they do not reach out to the operational levels of a big department. Employment equity programs just churn out paper but never have an impact on the women who are actually confronting the barriers.

· · · · ·

Parachuting women into high positions does not work. There is less resentment with bringing women up the ranks, providing them with the necessary training to advance, letting them prove themselves not only to others but also to themselves.

· · · · ·

Quotas tend to devalue the currency.

Quotas tend to devalue the currency.

· · · · ·

Programs for women must be made less visible. There has been so much noise made about them that men are in revolt. In this sense, they have done more harm than good.

· · · · ·

I believe that it is generally not in women's interests to draw attention to the fact that they are female, except in some individual cases where formal means must be used to right a wrong. It would be counter-productive to force the appointment of women to positions for which they are not ready. However, I am strongly in favour of providing women (and men) with the opportunities to broaden their experience so that they will be prepared for promotion.

· · · · ·

Women might be put into jobs before they are really ready in order to meet a quota; to have a token woman.

· · · · ·

Whether it's true or not, men are left with the feeling that women need crutches. They can't make it on their own. That's a devastating thing to do to women.

· · · · ·

Women who are promoted are often viewed with resentment and suspicion. Others assume they are there only because they are a woman rather than based on their abilities and qualifications. Women are often given a hard time after they are promoted until they prove that they can do the job well.

· · · · ·

56

The Government has made a tremendous mistake by promoting people to a large extent because they were a member of a target group as opposed to having the right qualifications to cope with the position. Having done that, the Government now has to offer support systems and training to those people so that they can grow in their jobs.

· · · · ·

With respect to affirmative action programs, don't take the PS as a whole. Determine where progress can be made and spend time identifying those areas where women are interested. Make sure to appoint competent women to positions and, especially, leave them long enough in order to earn respect from their male colleagues; this is the only way to change deeply held perceptions and prejudices. There should be less concentration on quotas, knowing that the public service is struggling in the midst of many restraints.

· · · · ·

Another double-bind women face is the male backlash and belief that women are being promoted by virtue of being female. If they do not get promoted, it is because their work is not good enough. If they do, it is only because they are female.

· · · · ·

You have to have your head in the sand not to know and recognize that, for several years, it has been the men who are being discriminated against.

· · · · ·

As far as personal experiences are concerned, I can honestly say that after 20 years with Revenue Canada and working in a number of diverse environments, I have never been aware of any obstacles or barriers to the advancement of women. In fact, recently my perception has been that the opposite is true.

· · · · ·

Many men feel that they are now the victims of "reverse discrimination" because of employment equity programs. They believe that preferential treatment is being given to women and Francophones in competitions, training and other promotional opportunities. As a result men are beginning to feel threatened and are resentful of equity programs.

· · · · ·

I realized that as a white, Anglo male I would have to be good to advance, because I would be competing against a lot of people — women; natives; Francophones.

· · · · ·

I don't think that quotas work. People learn how to play the game with numbers.

• • • • •

My biggest concern about quotas is that they want token numbers. The Government can hide behind that, use it to demonstrate all that they are doing. I mean, they probably think that they are doing the right thing.

• • • • •

You must have a demonstration effect. Whether you're talking about native Canadians, whether you're talking about women, black Americans, you must give the confidence that "my kind of person" can rise to the top in this establishment. Quotas are the least desirable but sometimes a necessary way of doing this. If you can't do it any other way, do it by quotas, and quotas may be quite useful to use as an ultimate sanction... I don't think any responsible manager wants to either impose them or use them but if that's the way you get there, that's the way you get there.

• • • • •

Every dog has its day. In the 1970s Francophones were promoted. Then it was women's turn. Now Treasury Board is working on a visible minority policy. Being a woman in the 1990s won't be as important. That's in the nature of things.

• • • • •

Attitudes are changing but these things take time. Employment equity programs should ultimately disappear as the service hires more women at all levels. There has been some backlash from men. There are men who have been done out of a promotion by employment equity thrusts, but this happens less now that women have proved their stripes. There has been a natural evolution in attitudes. Men make fewer blatant sexist comments now, at least out loud. Although this has not reached the ideal situation yet, even this is an improvement because men receive less reinforcement now and do not promulgate their prejudices. This is an important step toward better attitudes towards women.

(12) SUICIDE JOBS
When opportunity knocks you had better take it, even if it is an opportunity to the Gates of Hell.

• • • • •

(Employers with their first female senior staff) are so keen and excited that they start pushing them into things. Women don't see the pitfalls; they can very easily get carried away with all this enthusiasm and

When opportunity knocks you had better take it, even if it is an opportunity to the Gates of Hell.

forget to be aware of their capabilities and limits. If you get pushed
into something that is beyond you and fall flat on your face, that's it
— You fall all by yourself.

• • • • •

There's nothing worse than to be in a position and not really sure you
can do the job, because you're there to look good. If you work to establish rapport and a team attitude with your fellows, it can be blown
apart when you're picked and parachuted. You have to compete at
the same level they all do.

• • • • •

After seeking my superior's opinion re my lack of success in competitions, he suggested that I should perhaps spend more time at home
with my child. It seemed that my fate was sealed right then and there.
He concluded that I had an attitude problem and should be removed.
In an internal letter about my case was written "I do not think we
have clear grounds for dismissal. We share some of the blame because
we put a relatively inexperienced supervisor in an office with
three unknown personalities and failed to recognize the potential
problem and provide for it."

• • • • •

Within the public service there is tremendous inertia reflected in the
attitude "Why should you get ahead?" Between the numbers game
and the inability to get rid of deadwood, it is next to impossible to
make room for the up-and-coming people. To get around this I've
taken several high-risk jobs: men often will not take these jobs. Also,
you may be set up for failure. The key is to clue in quickly, acknowl-
edge that it is an impossible job to your superiors and colleagues
and use humour to make the best of it. It is not necessarily a
no-win situation.

(13) FRONTIER JOBS
Women set up new initiatives and then they are turned over to Mr.
Manager to run.

• • • • •

My experience and skills have been used by the institution to get several programs established and running and then when it came time to
give credit where it was due ... the tasks were taken from me and
passed on to someone at a higher level.

*Women set up
new initiatives
and then they
are turned
over to
Mr. Manager
to run.*

(14) MORALE

Morale is a terrible problem in the public service right now. People are working 12-13 hour days. They don't see the light at the end of the tunnel and I think if those problems were addressed, then the question of opportunities for women would fall into line. There are barriers period in the public service. We don't have a good plan for career development. We don't have a good plan or strategy as to what the public service will be.

• • • • •

I was completely demoralized, concluded that there was no future for me in the federal government and became a leaver. I left Ottawa for British Columbia with no specific prospects and no security. I took a cut in pay of almost 30% when I accepted a position in trade policy with the BC government.

• • • • •

I think some of the barriers today are worse than they were when I was coming up. When I was coming up through the system there were a lot of jobs. Life was different in the 1960s and 1970s and the job opportunities were everywhere. So if you were willing to work hard and if you were willing to accept that there was an attitude problem, which I did, then there were jobs out there. I feel sorry for the younger women. We have women in this department who are well-educated but the job opportunities just aren't there. There are no resources to implement developmental programs. I think that one of the biggest barriers there is right now is the lack of developmental opportunities and new challenges.

• • • • •

I was completely demoralized and became a leaver.

SECTION 4
Balancing Work and Family Responsibilities

Women are still the prime caregivers. I still don't think there's enough day-care. I still don't think that there are support systems for women to allow them to get ahead. I think women still do most of the home-making in the home. I don't think men have reached the point where they're doing equal work in the home. Some men are, but I think most men aren't. Women are tired, having to juggle a job and the family. That's still an impediment to getting ahead in their careers.

• • • • •

There have got to be much more supportive roles for us and I don't know how we can come to grips with it because men tend to go out after work and have a drink or a cup of coffee and nitter and natter and talk. They'll do that. We tend to have to rush home because we've got other priorities, another job waiting for us.

• • • • •

I think women tend to carry greater family responsibility than men and have been more supportive of their husbands than husbands have been of wives. If the husband gets a promotion, the wife is more apt to adapt her career, whereas there aren't many men who would do the same thing for their wives.

• • • • •

Right now, we've got mechanical solutions coming out of our ears. We've got action programs, we've got this, we've got that. But nothing is being done with the real problems in the so-called "softer" areas, which are not so soft. Can we underestimate the importance of child-bearing and child-rearing to women? Women endure increasing stress from conflict between their jobs and their family responsibilities, and society still requires women to accept those responsibilities.

• • • • •

A lot of my male colleagues are married to very intelligent women who have careers while their husbands are stationed in Ottawa. When their husbands go abroad they abandon their career. But that isn't an obstacle put in by the system, it's a societal phenomenon. The foreign service is probably one of the worst organizations as far as making family adjustments to suit a career.

* * * * *

I had to make it clear to them that while I was interested in jobs abroad, I was not prepared to live apart from my family. And I have not deviated from that position and I don't foresee that I will deviate from that position. My experience in this department is that all the women who are heads of mission, with perhaps one exception, are single women. They have neither husbands nor children. I find it unacceptable that only single women can be accommodated within the system that we have. I've made it clear to them that I will not operate as though I were a single women.

* * * * *

Successful foreign service women have been conditioned to think that they really can't have a normal family life and be a successful foreign service woman. Now that has to reduce the appeal of life in the foreign service. We must start seeing women with normal family lives progress through the department, through jobs abroad. No decisions have been made about how to find jobs for the spouses of employees who are sent abroad. Some of my male colleagues have wives who feel quite put upon by having to go abroad. The foreign service doesn't have anything where they make a real effort to help spouses find jobs abroad.

* * * * *

I sometimes wonder about this phrase "Having it all" because in my experience it's not having it all, it's doing it all. You have to do it all and it's all in the way you do it. It seems to me that nobody has ever successfully come out of this organization without having some kind of arrangement that made them feel comfortable about raising their children.

* * * * *

If you admit you are having problems coping with family and a career then you are considered unprofessional. I still think we have a very long way to go before the caring dimension of life is legitimate in business, career and any other dimension of life.

* * * * *

I sometimes wonder about this phrase "Having it all" because in my experience it's not having it all, it's doing it all.

My colleague and I were discussing two employees and sort of extolling the virtues of these two women. My colleague noticed that although these two women have children, we had never really heard them discuss their children in the office. They keep their family totally away from the office and when they're here they're professionals. The fact that these women are mothers makes you admire them even more. They've managed to juggle the two.

· · · · ·

I went to talk to them (men at a conference) about employment equity and you should have heard them, they all thought it was a bloody joke. "I would like to have my wife's job. All she does is play tennis and golf." I said, "That's nice, so you think that because you have a traditional family, which is only 15% of all families, that you should expect that everyone else does?" They don't understand that I am married with three children and know what I am talking about.

· · · · ·

I know damn well that I probably work much harder than most of my male counterparts. I don't come in until nine o'clock but I also didn't get here at seven-thirty, have my coffee and paper delivered to me; and I don't go home and have my paper ready for me while someone cooks up my meal. I'm not looking for special treatment, but don't make life so difficult when I have to go home to my family.

· · · · ·

Quite frankly there is a period of time when physically and mentally you have to make some trade-offs between your children and your career. When I was raising my children I simply could not have coped with the kind of career I have now or had before my first child. I believe it is really possible to make part-time arrangements for people with children.

· · · · ·

My advice to young women starting out on a career is ... to get your career moving before you take on a lot of other responsibilities such as children. I don't think you can consider yourself a success if you neglect your family to concentrate on a career. You have to look after your whole life. I think there has been a recent change in values as far as careers go. I think people are investing less of their hopes into a career. People look more at the quality of life and so they look to outside activities. I think people want a more rounded life and I'm glad to see that.

· · · · ·

I still think we have a very long way to go before the caring dimension of life is legitimate in business.

You can't say a woman is not successful, she has just done other things.

A woman who wants to have her family and keep her job, but work reduced hours, is not going to advance as quickly as a man who didn't take a day off. But when the woman returns full-time she will get these opportunities again. You have to look at the whole picture of what a woman wants to accomplish. You can't say a woman is a failure or not successful, she has just done other things. And I don't think a career is the only thing in a woman's life.

• • • • •

Another attitude problem is the feeling of employers that women are not very dependable because they have the extra responsibility of looking after children. So if their child is sick, it is usually the wife, not the husband, who stays home and looks after the child. That makes her less dependable as far as her job goes. Because there have been experiences like that, employers tend to distrust women.

• • • • •

I think the Government has to recognize the time has come that there will be women that need some sort of support just to help us get through.

• • • • •

The pecking order is changing more quickly than the social supports for women who are rising in it.

• • • • •

As I progressed into my career more of the barriers became things like child care. I mean, I come to work and end up doing three or four hours worth of work before I get here because of all the child care.

• • • • •

I do believe that there is a really radical shift in priorities on the part of women. But I think that society still does its dastardly deed on women where I have seen the husbands become the most conservative when children enter the picture. It's going to be a long, long time before that changes in any significant way.

• • • • •

Should a woman not have any children, or forget the ones she has?

• • • • •

SECTION 5
Coping Strategies

(1) MARKETING

You need a sense of your own strengths and weaknesses, and it's easier for people to help you and work with you if you know what you want to do. You have to do a good job. You have to build a track record, stay in a job long enough to earn credibility. You have to focus yourself, and build a constituency outside the public service. If you can do that, you modify the power structure; people see you do a job that women traditionally haven't done.

· · · · ·

When you have an individual with drive and capacity, and they have an opportunity and they seize it, at that point you get accomplishment. The individual must also have a certain amount of intelligence, a desire to succeed and an ability to learn as you go along.

· · · · ·

I would encourage women to learn how to think as leaders, to watch how people get things done, to learn from the good examples around them and to be interested in what is going on around them. So when we have developmental assignments in line management or operational management then we know that there are women out there who are interested.

· · · · ·

University training is important. Strong interpersonal skills are extremely important: great flexibility, and the ability to analyze the power structure and make alliances with peers and subordinates, especially key men.

· · · · ·

The way I approached unacceptable job offers was not to say that I was insulted by them, but to tell them that I would look into it and get back to them. Then I did my homework and went back to them and

You could run faster and faster in smaller and smaller circles, but life is full of tomorrow mornings.

thanked them for thinking of me. I also told them the reasons I was not interested in the job. In every case I really made a serious effort to see what the situation was. Gradually the offers started to get better and then I had to make a more careful judgement about whether or not it would be a good career move for me.

· · · · ·

I learned to analyze the job description, I learned to associate it with my work experience and I learned to talk with some of the managers involved before the board so they understood how personally interested I was. I started to do a compendium of the most interesting questions. I learned to keep track of these things. I finally reached a position where I was very confident going into boards, just based on the work I had done.

· · · · ·

It's women who are very bright, very motivated and who are killing themselves because they're trying to do it all, and I guess sometimes my advice to them is, go home and have a really long chat with the mirror and see what your real priorities are for this five-year period.

· · · · ·

Part of your value has to do with distance, has to do with humour, has to do with knowledge in a wide variety of areas, and yes, you could run faster and faster in smaller and smaller circles and you could certainly get the Cabinet document produced for tomorrow morning. It would have been a better decision not to go to the theatre, it would have been a better decision to work on the Cabinet document, but life is full of tomorrow mornings.

· · · · ·

What I had was a very basic idea that in order to succeed I had to really be very good. My idea was that professional excellence was the key to any form of career. I haven't really had a very good political coping strategy, I've had a very simplistic view, I have had the view that if I work hard and do extremely well that I can overcome barriers.

· · · · ·

It is basically human management you see. It is knowing how to develop a vision for where you want to be in five years of service and knowing what are the pitfalls.

(2) NETWORKING

Women are still a relative minority, so they still encounter barriers to the exercise of power. Women are left out of networks, because the boys get together in places where women don't go. I joke about conversations in women's washrooms, but a sort of critical mass is reached there. Once there are enough women, they're going to be brought into decision-making. Traditional networks will have to change, and incorporate the women.

· · · · ·

I think women must continue to be supportive with each other. They have to get together and determine what kind of a difference they want to make and what kind of a federal civil service they want to have. And have it. And make it happen.

(3) MENTORS

I have several mentors and I think that this is a great strength. If several people in your business believe in you and think of you and expect you to do well, you have a lot of people standing up for you, putting your name forward and calling on you if they see something they think you may be interested in. The more people that are highly thought of and think highly of you, the better.

· · · · ·

I had a mentor who was very very helpful to me. I learned so much from her in terms of strategies, approaches and how to deal with people.

· · · · ·

Most importantly, I learned about group dynamics from my mentor. She was always pointing out why something worked and why another thing did not. She was a natural coach and charged her prodigies with being coaches too. I have this role now.

· · · · ·

As you are progressing up the ladder in the public service it is really important to have someone at a higher level who you can use as a sounding board for your ideas and questions. Unfortunately, the majority of people in these higher level positions are still men and they are understandably wary of becoming mentors to women because of the potential for office gossip. Upwardly mobile men do not have this problem.

· · · · ·

I think mentors are very, very important. It's somebody who takes a specific interest in you. That happens less and less as you get into the higher levels. You almost have to have a male mentor because there aren't any women in the higher jobs around here.

· · · · ·

If you're serious about a career in the public service, sit for the first year and just observe, really sponge up everything around you. There is a very intricate way of doing things, rules, regulations, procedures and policies. Decide where you want to go, and find out how to get there. If there is no clear path, find a high-up, respected person who's been around and who you can communicate with and trust, and make a proposal. Say "This is what I can do, and here are the steps that I have to take to do it."

· · · · ·

A competent woman working for a competent boss "shines." Her reputation and credibility become better established and she becomes better known and able to use the "old boys' network," still one of the most important ways to obtain challenging and substantive job assignments.

· · · · ·

It is important to provide women with informal "mentors" early on in their career and to assign them into jobs where they work for some of the more successful (and sympathetic) officers in the department.

· · · · ·

It is almost systematizing the mentor system because there is no question that women don't have access to mentors, men have.

· · · · ·

One thing I'll always regret is not pursuing a senior women, who was trying to be a mentor to me. I didn't know about mentors at the time. She really helped me find my place but wasn't the sort to push herself on you, but she did what she could to help me. There were others who helped me, sometimes helping me when I really realized I needed help. It gradually dawned on me that I was getting help and I tried to help others. I realize now that I always had persons as mentors.

· · · · ·

I always learned from people around me — either from my direct superior or from colleagues who were not my superiors, but who were in a more senior position. That's how I learned.

· · · · ·

When I was a young woman in Winnipeg I had the good fortune to become associated with a small group of women, all of whom were doing interesting things. They certainly kept me from getting rusty when I was at home with small children.

· · · · ·

I've the support of people who have been almost like elder brothers, which is what I mean by mentor. I've been able to watch their management style, they have taken an interest in me and pushed me to move ahead. They gave me advice on how I might better prepare myself for anything — and that's very critical.

• • • • •

In each place that I work I try to pick one person who is obviously better and more experienced than I am for a mentor. In some cases it's my immediate boss. Sometimes though, when you have a good rapport with someone who is a mentor to you, people will assume that there is a sexual relationship.

• • • • •

(Talking about a colleague in a senior administrative post) She has recently moved out of the shadow of a man that she had worked closely with for a long time. And it wasn't until he left that she was really able to blossom. They worked very well together, and were mutually very supportive of one another as long as he was there relying on her, which didn't leave much room for her to grow. It was a problem.

• • • • •

You usually don't follow a mentor through a logical path. I think having mentors works for people because it teaches them new skills and builds confidence.

• • • • •

On the mentor issue, I think what the woman has to do is say "Well, I have grown as far as I can grow under this man, it is time for me to spread my wings."

• • • • •

I think a lot of women develop through mentors, which can at a certain stage be detrimental to a woman. It is difficult to jump over and become parallel to your mentors.

(4) ROLE MODELS

The man that was assigned to me was really positive and supportive in everything, always saying that I can do anything.

• • • • •

I did not have a mentor, but I did work with some people who were very highly respected in this place. I was very well trained. When I came back from my first posting I worked for a person I consider to be

They gave me advice on how I might better prepare myself for anything — and that's very critical.

one of the best officers in this part. Working for him was a great advantage because it taught me a lot. I think it gave me great credibility having worked for him.

• • • • •

I have to give my boss full credit for an excellent personnel policy where he's looking at people two and three years ahead. And that's the way he does it. He is very concerned about human resource development and, I mean, it shows. All of the three people who are involved in the decentralization of this branch have been involved in the programs for a long time and he's made sure, for example, that I have someone working with me now who will be my lifeline in the future.

• • • • •

One man I worked for said to get a file folder, put FUTURE on the front and always be thinking of it.

One man I worked for was really great. He said, "Now what I think you should do is get a file folder, put FUTURE on the front of it, stick it in your drawer and always be thinking of it and looking at opportunities down the road." I've had co-op students since and I say the same thing. I think he was truly concerned about my future, ahead of his own at that point. It's in human nature to wish the best for someone else as long as it doesn't affect your own future. But he was able to do it.

• • • • •

The editor was a marvelous person to work for, brilliant and interesting. He pushed me to do what I could, rather than hold me back.

• • • • •

I was very lucky because my first boss in the public service was a man ... and if it hadn't been for him I would never have gone for a promotion, and I would never have developed interests and the confidence, I don't think, to have had such a good career and have so much fun.

• • • • •

A colleague of mine was a very nurturing person. He tried to develop the people that worked for him, which I think is very important. I think that a lot more directors should have this quality. I was very young and he would make sure that I was involved in meetings and would make sure that I knew that I was supposed to be there. It certainly had a positive effect on me. And it wasn't just because I was a woman. He would have done the same thing for anyone.

• • • • •

Women are human beings to my boss. Through my work with him I think I was able to gain my self-esteem, regain it in fact, because it had really been whittled away over the years. The first performance appraisal I got came through the mail! Signed by people I hardly knew.

• • • • •

There's a fellow that I've worked with who has been particularly good. In a way he makes a joke of the situation, saying for example, "She's my boss" in a way that sort of sounds like "Can you believe that she's my boss?" Nonetheless he still gets the message through and he's made it very easy for me in that regard because he's a captain's rank and there he is. Men immediately turn to him and he'll turn to me and do as I say.

$$* \quad * \quad * \quad * \quad *$$

(In a letter to the college council) I said that I thought it was time for the college to take a stand on the degradation of women on the campus and three days later (the principal) came around to every single trades trainee in the classroom and said that this kind of sexist action and language is inappropriate in an institute of higher learning. If it continues you will be thrown out of school and you will not get an apprenticeship anywhere in (the province).

(5) OPTING OUT

... our health and personal lives suffer. The brass ring tastes lousy.

$$* \quad * \quad * \quad * \quad *$$

I think I was earning maybe $10, $12 thousand, (with 20-25 years of experience) and the men were earning maybe $20 thousand. The natural question would be, "Why aren't you quitting?" The men would say, "Oh, but I have a mortgage and I have a pension plan and I have all of these responsibilities." So I started an "F You" fund. And it was a chunk of money, it started out with $2 thousand and basically allowed me at any time to get up and say, "Okay, I give up. F you." I've used it once.

$$* \quad * \quad * \quad * \quad *$$

I was told by the director general in question that I wasn't qualified for the job and I knew perfectly well that I was and he had not had an opportunity anyway to look at my résumé or my experience. It was a purely reactionary statement that I was certain was a glass ceiling and it happened again at Treasury Board Secretariat. I haven't had it happen since then. I left.

(6) HURDLES

Eventually you start feeling that the barriers were just hurdles or irritants and because you conquered them you forget them. You ignore the people that are verbally cruel or discriminated against you. You take the attitude that you are not going to let that bother you and you overcome it and rise above it.

$$* \quad * \quad * \quad * \quad *$$

... our health and personal lives suffer. The brass ring tastes lousy.

I think that accepting defeat or thinking that there is nothing you can do about a situation is a big barrier. Young men and women must be taught how to solve problems and how to come up with analytical solutions to the barriers they encounter.

· · · · ·

In a study done at the Harvard Business School about how women and men's views are handled, they found that when a woman says something a lot of people ignore it, but when a man says the same thing, everybody thinks it's a great idea. I see that. But my approach is to keep repeating it, or find some man to say it. I make allies, and eventually I get through. Things like that are barriers, but I find ways to get around them.

· · · · ·

I don't have the problem, they do; I refuse to take on their problems.

When I was a broadcaster I had to tell the producer what to do and he didn't like it and I wondered "How do you do it?" Do I put my foot down and tell him I'm the boss? Do I try to seduce him into doing what I want him to do? I decided that I wasn't going to seduce him and I wasn't going to put my foot down either but I was going to gradually affirm myself and have rational discussions with him on how I thought it should be done ... and so I found my way of exercising my authority and it was between these two options.

· · · · ·

I was a young woman, and to make it worse, I did not look like everybody else. For an employer I am a double whammy, a black woman; I learned at a very early age not to wonder if they are concerned about my religion, my colour or my sex, because I cannot be bothered if I don't make it my problem. I don't have the problem, they do; I refuse to take on their problems.

· · · · ·

It's not that I see it as a battle, I just see it as people trying to tell me what to do; being a spunky kid, I have to make up my own mind because I **have** got one.

· · · · ·

I had no role models in my work. As a housewife I knew what had to be done, and from my first job I set my own standards. I'm a pusher and a go-getter. In spite of my boss's objections, I got licensed for both the forklift and the three-ton truck. My boss, maybe because he didn't want to give me any more favours than he had already, didn't want to give in to me at the start and put me down, but you know, I had to move on to different things.

· · · · ·

You have to make sure that you get a little bit of the spotlight around here. You don't have to be arrogant, sometimes you can do it by simply making a funny comment. Or sometimes you can do it by making a perceptive interjection. But you have to sell yourself. People have to recognize you as a force and you have to put yourself in circumstances where you get that recognition.

· · · · ·

But again, my perverse sense of humor came through and I wasn't going to back down, and I thought, "They've got me and they're stuck with me. I'll go in as if I am really wanted here."

· · · · ·

I know they don't think that fire halls are the proper place for women but they don't say so to my face. And I am not going to get into it with them, there is absolutely no point in that; I am pleasant to them and they are to me.

· · · · ·

My approach in all these jobs has been to go in and do a good job, do what I think has to be done, and follow my instincts. Inevitably they come around, because they see that I'm quite competent and that I will listen to them and make my own judgements. If some continue to harbour hostility, that's their problem, not mine.

· · · · ·

For 15 to 20 years there have been strugglers coming up, and you might think of me as one of them. I have found my little upward path by being as pleasant as I can in speaking to the world. I really don't get mad at people when they do mean things because I feel sorry for them. I go under or sideways around people who obstruct me; I am not blocked but just diverted, for I never take my eye off the goal post. I find my way honestly. I don't mind hard work.

· · · · ·

I was labelled an aggressive bitch and I knew who was saying it. So I picked up the phone and called them and said, "I have heard some rumors, but I knew that you would never say those things. I mean, you're my colleague and I just know that you wouldn't say them. But I think it's really important that you know that you are being quoted that way." They said, "Of course you're right. Of course we wouldn't say those things." That's been most effective, going back. Always take the high road on this sort of thing.

· · · · ·

You have to make sure that you get a little bit of the spotlight around here.

I am not blocked but just diverted, for I never take my eye off the goal post.

First of all, I believe very strongly that if one goes out and meets people who have these (negative) attitudes and opens up dialogue with them and demonstrates that good results can be achieved, that good results will still be achieved and that is the way I dealt with it by maintaining the dialogue by working with people and by delivering the expected results.

· · · · ·

I always meant to be the boss, but I didn't aim to be this boss or any particular boss.

· · · · ·

I think first of all every woman who is going to be in this sort of situation has got to have a good balance in that she must have absolute confidence in her ability to do the job. And one must have the courage, and it is truly courage, to face down that very difficult feat of identifying which is really a form of prejudice and stare it down and deal with it. It's important that one not be intimidated by the fact that one is fairly certain that some people are thinking that the job cannot be done by a woman or that some people are thinking the job should not be done by a woman. So I think that the first thing that one really has to have is an absolutely superb sense of humour. And, dare I say this, I think that it has to be said that women have to be really comfortable with their own sexuality, so that one is not uncomfortable when men's behaviour might potentially embarrass some women.

· · · · ·

SELECTED
CASE
STUDIES

Lynn Young

CURRENT SITUATION

Lynn Young is currently the District Manager, Labour Canada, Capital Regional Office (PM-6) responsible for the operational planning and management of the labour affairs officers in the region and the management of the office itself. The district staff includes nine people. The position reports to the Regional Director of the Capital Region.

Lynn started in this position in the fall of 1988. She found the first four months a real learning experience and "a bit frustrating." She has an extensive background in the Department (virtually her entire career was in the Department), however, this is the first time she has been in a line management position.

She sees her strengths as management, and recognizes that she does not have the technical background of the officers she supervises. She needs to draw on their expertise and apply her own judgement and common sense.

CAREER PATH

1972

Lynn completed commercial secondary education in the early 1970s in Ottawa. Her education included a work term in the federal public service and subsequent opportunities for full-time employment, organized through the school.

Lynn joined the public service directly out of high school in the typing pool at the Department of the Solicitor General (ST-3). The school placed the top ten students. While she took the PSC tests (typing, dictation), she did not have a formal interview.

She moved to Labour Canada in response to a referral generated from her initial application to the public service. This position was at the same level but was a better position in that it was at the branch level. Getting out of the typing pool could have been much harder.

I always had the attitude of doing what the organization needs.

Lynn is bilingual and was able to do shorthand in both official languages. She considers that these skills were crucial in her first jobs. She was "marketable."

Subsequently, Lynn applied for and won promotions to SCY-1 and SCY-2 positions. Over this period, she also transferred through the Department, widening her perspective and learning new skills. She always went beyond her job description to learn new skills that might help her later on in her career. For example, in one SCY position she did not have mail responsibilities. Nevertheless, she learned how to handle the incoming mail, classifying the documents and thus learning the filing system. This knowledge and experience was beneficial in a subsequent competition.

1976

Lynn won an AS-1 developmental position. The Department set aside five PYs for this program. She recalls that there was an eligible list established with 20 names. The first five (including Lynn) received positions immediately. These were floating positions, six-month assignments. As these individuals moved into "regular" positions, more people were appointed from the list.

During the course of this program, Lynn worked in official languages and in the labour data collection areas on assignment.

1977

The Department was decentralizing, establishing regional offices. Lynn had known the regional directors through her branch involvement. She had the option of going either to Toronto or Montreal. She and her husband decided to move to Toronto, partly for personal reasons (her husband was an Anglophone). She considers this "the best move of my life." It was a gamble. There was no guarantee of a permanent position but she was not too worried. She felt confident something would come up.

This position involved working on all aspects of establishing the regional office, working closely with the Chief of Administration (Mary). Whenever Lynn was asked if she could perform a particular duty, she replied yes. She stretched herself constantly. This helped to build her confidence. Among other things, she participated in designing and implementing the assignment system for labour affairs officers (LAOs) and later was involved in the automation of the system.

1978

When Mary left to assume a PG position in Environment, Lynn was appointed to replace her as an AS-3 (acting). This was a second big opportunity. Lynn recalls being "very scared" over the first year or so. The position carried a great deal of responsibility: processing all the claims, signing under Section 26 of the *Financial Administration Act*, influencing personnel decisions. She was in the acting position for a year before a competition was run.

1980

Lynn won the AS-4, Head of Administration in the Ontario Regional Office. The position involved doing work plans, forecasting work-loads, preparing budgets and doing trend analysis, some of which was outside the scope of the job description. Again, she stretched her role. "I always had the attitude of doing what the organization needs."

1982

Both she and her husband felt they needed a change. They decided to return to Ottawa. Lynn realized she would have to go back to Ottawa to get ahead as she really did not want to be an LAO. She initiated the move. Gary McKnight, who is now her regional director, was at head-quarters and looking for someone. She transferred back. "The Department is really good that way, in accommodating people." She worked in the ADM's office, co-ordinating budgets, Treasury Board submissions and work plan analyses. Her regional experience was an asset. She worked on establishing a system to monitor performance indicators. This was a "fun job." She realized how much she liked analysis.

The environment in the branch offered opportunities to grow. It was a new structure with a new Assistant Deputy Minister. The ADM was very demanding but Lynn learned a lot from her, especially regarding the philosophy of the Department. She was already familiar with operations and the broader perspective was an excellent complement. The position was relatively high profile. She dealt with the minister, the deputy minister and all the regional directors.

Ultimately, after two years, she was concerned that the position was a dead end. The ADM had tried, unsuccessfully, to reclassify the position. Lynn "started to get panicky," wondering whether this is what she wanted to do for the rest of her life. She reviewed her experiences and her strengths. She recognized that she had considerable personnel experience and contacted the Personnel Branch asking them "not to forget me" if they needed someone. A while later they called her.

CASE STUDY 1   79

1984

She transferred to Personnel as an AS-4 in a PE-3 position. She negotiated to protect her AS-4 level while she took the staffing and classification certification training required to become a PE generalist. At the time, she viewed the training in Personnel as a means of ultimately moving to another department. Her career plan was to move out of Labour Canada and get experience in other government departments. She feels she learned a great deal during this period. She preferred the staffing role where she felt she truly helped managers. Classification was more of a control role, in her opinion.

Lynn stayed at the AS-4 level throughout this period. She achieved certification in staffing and is half way through the classification training.

1986

Gary McKnight called to ask her to work with him setting up the new Capital Region. While she liked the idea of working with Gary again, and especially the challenge of setting up a new region from scratch, she recognized that it was a step away from the PE direction she had been pursuing. She agreed to transfer over, negotiating for a two-year assignment, including LAO training. She never did get the LAO training, as it turned out.

1988

The position of District Manager (PM-5) opened up. The statement of qualifications was written to recognize related experience other than just LAO experience. This fact was not easily accepted by some of the LAOs who competed, but the backlash was limited. Lynn was successful in winning the position.

1989

Her position was reclassified (PM-6) and Lynn was promoted.

Lynn feels she has been very well accepted in the office. Her team-oriented style helps. In contrast, she thinks her predecessor was not proactive. Lynn developed work plans that were more proactive, and the staff have appreciated this. She expects to stay in this position at least four years.

TURNING POINTS

Looking back, Lynn saw a number of turning points in her career:

- winning the AS-1 developmental position;
- moving to Toronto;
- acting appointment to the AS-3 level;
- moving to the Personnel Branch;
- moving to Ottawa regional office; and
- winning the PM-5 competition.

PERCEIVED BARRIERS

Lynn identified the following barriers to women in the public service:

- Lack of career planning at the individual level and human resource planning at a more macro level. Lynn points out that every move she made was on her own. No one opens any doors in the public service.
- In the public service staffing process, potential does not count for much. The way in which the merit principle is interpreted in most departments is you have to have done the job before you can get it.
- Lack of knowledge on how the staffing system works can be an impediment, especially at the very junior levels. She did not, at first, realize the link between the poster/statement of qualifications and how to apply for a job and prepare for an interview. Renée, a former supervisor, coached her in this. She, in turn, coaches her staff.
- The appraisal system supposedly identifies superior performers (high flyers) but appraisals do not seem to have much impact in staffing.
- The lack of bridging positions.
- Women's own lack of initiative: you have to go out and get what you want.

A woman who was on the developmental AS-1 program at the same time as Lynn, remarked that there are male managers who stereotype women. For example, because she was once a secretary, she is still occasionally asked to stay late to type a report. She feels some managers cannot get beyond the fact that you were once a secretary. Consequently, it is difficult to get these managers to welcome your comments in a serious manner.

A peer of Lynn's in Personnel reflected that the size of the Department can be a barrier. The Department is relatively small and thus there are fewer senior positions. He stated that the Department lacks PYs to expand and thus is perhaps "destined to be small."

On the other side of the coin, another colleague in the Department pointed out that a small department can be both a barrier and a facilitator for career progression. If a department is small, he reflected that it is easier to identify "bright lights" and if a person is doing a good job, more people will be aware of this fact. For example, in a smaller department, officers can have more occasion to deal directly with higher levels of management, such as the ADM, on a regular basis.

BALANCING FAMILY AND CAREER

Lynn is currently separated with no children. She considered having children when she first returned to Ottawa. At that time, she felt she was ready to "coast" a bit and could afford the time investment in having a child. It just did not happen. When she did not have children, she had more energy to devote to her career.

Her move to Toronto was partially influenced by her husband's desire to broaden his career options. It was a good move for both of them at that point in their careers.

PERCEIVED FACILITATORS

Lynn identified these facilitators in her career progression and in the progression of other women:
* bridging positions;
* good mentors and supervisors; and
* networking.

Lynn has worked to establish bridging positions. For example, while in Toronto she was instrumental in creating a PM-1 position that has subsequently moved three support/junior staff into LAO positions and also an AS-1 position back-up to the AS-4 Head, Administration.

She was very complimentary about the Department's program that offered her her first big break. Apparently, the Department set aside five PYs each year for a number of years in the 1970s. Lynn believes that 20 people benefited from this process, a very significant percentage in a small department.

A colleague of Lynn's, who was also placed on the Department's development program, explained that the program was open to support staff "with potential." This individual, Kathy, was a secretary at the time and the program allowed her the opportunity to gain valuable work experience. The program itself was 18 months in duration and Kathy spent a year in the Women's Bureau and six months in Finance, where she accepted a permanent position upon completion of the program. Kathy remarked that this program gave support staff, perhaps without a formal education, the opportunity to grow in work experience. "The program was beneficial and proved to the Department that support staff are capable, trainable employees." Kathy has remained with Labour Canada.

SELF-ASSESSMENT

Lynn noted the need for individuals to realistically assess their strengths and weaknesses in the process of career planning. Lynn assessed her strengths and weaknesses as follows:

* management skills;
* bilingual;
* hard working;
* visibility (did not get buried);
* will probably need some further education to advance beyond this level;
* broad knowledge of the mission/mandate of the Department coupled with good understanding of procedures/practices; and
* strong network within the Department.

Lynn likes Labour Canada very much, although, she recognizes that it is a small department and that further advancement might be limited without a broader perspective but she also feels very comfortable in the Department.

One of her strengths, her willingness and eagerness to take on challenges, to stretch herself, has been criticized by others: taking on too much, not learning to say no.

MENTORS

Lynn considers mentoring to be an essential feature in career planning and has tried to be a mentor to other staff, to pass on the assistance/coaching she received.

Lynn described her mentors and their contributions to her career:

* Renée was definitely a mentor. She encouraged Lynn to apply for the AS-1 competition. One of the assessment techniques in that competition was the preparation of a plan to establish an office. Candidates were given a week to prepare their plans and had to present to the board. Lynn practised her presentation with Renée, who gave her some good coaching. By the time she presented to the board, she felt very confident.

Mary, the AS-4 in Toronto when she was an AS-1, coached Lynn and involved her in a wide range of activities. Mary identified Lynn as her replacement when she left. "She convinced the Regional Director to try me." At that time, Lynn acknowledges she was "green" but Mary must have seen her potential. This caused some resentment among other staff.

ROLE MODELS

Lynn regarded Mary as a role model. At a formative stage in Lynn's career she was able to observe Mary doing a very responsible job. It helped set her own aspirations.

Lynn also looked at a former ADM as a role model. This woman was a very senior woman in the Department making it clear that women could aspire to senior executive positions.

NETWORKING

Lynn remarked that she has always networked to some extent. Even when she first entered the Department in support positions, she moved around and made contacts. Thus, she learned about the Department and the managers. Lynn reflects on the fact that she knows a lot of people in the Department well and has deliberately sought to maintain and enhance her network of contacts. She attributes her moves to Toronto, to personnel and then to the region to making contacts with people she knew, who also knew her reputation.

COLLEAGUES' PERSPECTIVES

In addition to the comments that have been integrated above, colleagues mentioned the following about Lynn's career and the Department:

- A human resource professional in the Department commented that one typical career path is from the clerical group into LAO training and then possibly eventually manager. Lynn's career has broken this traditional mold in the sense that she does not have LAO experience. "She is showing that it was a good move." Her move from Manager, Regional Service to District Manager was described by a colleague as "extraordinary" although initially unpopular.
- An individual who has known Lynn since the 1970s commented that she "can take on too much." He reflected that this could allow managers to take advantage of her ability and willingness to stretch herself. This characteristic has caused Lynn some personal stress.

- Lynn always made herself available for extra activities and responsibilities, particularly when she was in a support position. She exhibited a great sense of curiosity. A colleague remarked that many support people do not exhibit this quality and possess a mentality whereby they do the minimum work required and then go home. Unfortunately, these same individuals then complain about not being promoted.
- "Lynn was a visible performer who was in the right place at the right time." There is an element of luck in career progression.
- All colleagues agreed that Labour Canada was a good department in terms of training. "They have a good record at developing people." Unfortunately, the downsizing has limited this somewhat.

OTHER COMMENTS AND SUGGESTIONS
Lynn and her colleagues had the following comments and suggestions:
- Establish more bridging positions.
- Individuals must conduct good career planning; know your strengths and your likes and dislikes in a job.
- Teach women (and men) how the staffing system works.
- Place more government-wide emphasis on employees being given the opportunity to learn. Are they trainable? If so, give them the opportunity.
- When post-secondary education is stated as a requirement for a position, perhaps allow those without this formal education (but with work experience) to take an exam in lieu. This would allow these employees to get "a foot in the door."
- Women must be aware of the fine line between aggressive and assertive behaviour. Certain situations require aggressive behaviour, while others require assertive action. Know the difference.
- The broad picture is important for both men and women.
- More use of secondments and various transfer/assignment systems. These human resource mechanisms provide individuals with more diverse experience than would normally be available.
- Departments require creativity and flexibility in developing their staff.
- Do not let opportunities for development decrease due to financial restraint. PYs should not be less available to invest in development at the expense of immediate results. View staff development as an investment not as a cost.

CASE STUDY 2
Denise Morin

You cannot just sit around and whine about the lack of opportunity.

CURRENT SITUATION

Denise is currently the Acting Administrative Assistant in the personnel area in the Systems and Procedures Branch of the Canada Employment and Immigration Commission (AS-2). The branch includes about 400 people. Her work entails tracking person-years for the branch to avoid slippage, initiating staffing actions and other personnel administration.

Denise started this job in January 1989. She feels she is still in a learning mode but has already seen opportunities for streamlining the process. She heard about the opening through a friend who formerly held the position. The job required a strong personnel background, which she had with 18 years in the personnel area (staffing, pay and benefits, and staff relations, through the union). Her current supervisor is someone who was her supervisor previously; he was a staffing officer when she was a staffing assistant.

Her current supervisor notes that he chose Denise for this acting position because he was aware of her work habits (thorough, accurate, methodological), personnel experience, honesty and loyalty. In addition, he knew that her personality matched his, that she was a hard worker and, finally, that she was dissatisfied with where she was.

CAREER PATH

1960

After high school graduation, Denise began working as a clerk at Metropolitan Life, working her way up to a supervisory position. She had grown up in the Ottawa area. She considered working for the Government but, "in those days, women could not have a child and work in the public service."

1967
She moved to a smaller company, an insurance broker.

1970
She quit working for a year, in a bid to save her floundering marriage.

1971
Back on the job market, after the failure of her marriage, Denise moved to Toronto. She did not "know a soul" there but felt the need to break away. She worked a short time in a photo development shop then responded to an ad for administrative work at National Life. She knew insurance and was successful in obtaining the job right away. She remained in the job about a year but ultimately decided to move back to Ottawa. She wanted to be closer to her family. Indeed, she moved in with her aunt.

1972
At first, she did not feel any pressure to get a job. Her expenses were light as she was living with family. Finally, she decided to look for a job in Ottawa. She went to Manpower and was referred to the Unemployment Insurance Commission, Pay and Benefits Section as a CR-3. She was hired right away. Denise worked in Pay and Benefits a few months then moved to Manpower Planning for a couple of years.

1974
The staffing supervisor asked her to move to Staffing. Denise went there as a CR-4 and worked the next seven years as a Staffing Assistant. After a while, she realized she wanted to go further and applied twice for competitions to become a staffing officer. She met the knowledge and abilities criteria but not the personal suitability factors. It was explained to her that she "was not ready" for the work of a staffing officer and that it was "too big a jump." She had acted as a staffing officer for six months, doing the full load, "but with no recognition and no acting pay." In retrospect, Denise considers that part of the "problem" was her reputation for being outspoken, for calling "a spade a spade," and that management was concerned she would not adapt. They felt that she would not bend the rules.

Denise met the man she would marry about this time, and the "romance" took her mind off other things. She made a lot of life changes around this time and was "lazy about her career."

1980

When she did not get the staffing officer position, she applied to go on language training. She was successful on language training. When she returned, she asked for a transfer to another area.

1981

Denise began working in Pay and Benefits once again. She really liked this work, finding it particularly satisfying to respond to employee requests for information, a task that many of her peers did not like. According to Denise, the work was stimulating, "never a dull moment."

In this position, unlike earlier Personnel Branch positions, Denise was no longer excluded from collective bargaining. While she did not see herself as a unionist, in the old blue-collar style, she recognized the need for the union. She decided to get involved because she considered the current union executive, at the local level, was not meeting employees' needs. She was quickly elected Local President. It should be noted that these events occurred just after the CR strike in 1981.

1985

She was elected as the alternate National VP of the department component of PSAC. Denise believes that the union VP she worked with was excellent and that she learned a great deal from him.

1986

Denise took over as National VP of the component. In this role, she had a lot of interaction with senior managers/executives in the Department and learned not to be intimidated by them. She feels many clerks are intimidated by senior managers. She found the work very strenuous, and took it all very seriously. She considers that men often do these high visibility jobs with a view to their own advancement. She never gave that view much thought although she now realizes that the experience has positioned her well. She feels she learned a great deal about herself, her values and her convictions during this period. She realized that she had to maintain realism and balance in defending employees' interests.

1989

She made the decision to leave Pay and Benefits because there had been an AS-2 competition in the area, and the most junior person was selected over others with up to eight years experience. The position had always been "English only" but was staffed bilingual C-level imperative. The person who was selected for the job was a Francophone. The poster was only put out after this person had acted for eight months. This was the "straw that broke the camel's back" and she decided she could not go back to that group. Fortunately, the opportunity in the Systems and Procedures Branch came up at that time.

TURNING POINTS

Looking back, Denise saw a number of turning points in her career:

- The breakdown of her first marriage was a personal turning point that impacted on her career, spurring her decision to move away from Ottawa.
- Her failure to win the PE competitions signalled a barrier in that career path. It led to her move into Pay and Benefits.
- She considers that her union involvement was an excellent, invaluable experience. She took the training offered through the union. She feels she mastered a great deal during this period and that the activities truly "strengthened her, as a person." She learned how to run meetings, how to work with groups of people, how to handle grievances. Her approach was to try to be as objective as possible. She recognized the need to balance the concerns of the individual worker against the rest of the group.
- She considers the current acting AS-2 position to be her long-awaited big break. She had not been trying for a promotion recently, because other things had occupied her attention. "This is a real opportunity."

Ultimately, Denise sees herself becoming an executive assistant. She does not want to move towards a policy role.

PERCEIVED BARRIERS

From Denise's perspective, there are a number of barriers that confront women in the public service:

- Classification structure. There is a big gap between CR-4 and PE-3, for example, and very few bridging positions.
- Absence of a good, realistic appraisal process. The present appraisal process is wishy-washy. It does not provide valuable, realistic feedback. She points to her inability to win the PE-2 competitions. Her appraisals had never given any indication that she would not be suitable. She feels she "beat her head against a wall."

- Own perceived dislike of being a supervisor. She is not a "control-oriented" person and does not like having to scrutinize other people's work. She expressed the need for good training in supervisory skills. It should be noted that Denise's colleagues and former supervisor did not share her own view of her "lack" of supervisory skills. This discrepancy is particularly interesting in light of her comments about the appraisal system.
- Complete lack of career counselling. This is particularly noticeable in a department that is responsible for employment equity and for counselling workers.
- Getting too comfortable. A comfortable job can trap a person in a female job ghetto. She recognizes that there is a price to be paid to get ahead. "You have to take chances, invest a bit more of your time in things like outside courses. Men do this regularly and women have to do it too. You cannot just sit around and whine about the lack of opportunity. You have to make a decision and follow through." She points out that her own husband went back to university to complete his degree at night. Women have to do these things too.
- Staying too long in one job. This is an extension of the risk of being too comfortable. Denise feels she should have moved earlier. It is important to stretch yourself, to take on challenges if you want to get ahead.
- Family responsibilities. Denise has no children from her first marriage. A step-child from her second marriage (teenager) came to live with her and her husband in the early 1980s, thrusting her into a parenting role unexpectedly. She also has extended family responsibilities. Denise notes that her husband does his fair share of household work: cooking, cleaning, etc. She considers this sharing of chores to be a real advantage, commenting that women who insist on guarding their roles as "chief cook and bottle washer" at home inevitably do not have time to invest in their career. While this is a fair choice and should be respected, she feels that some women do not recognize the choices they are making.

One of her former supervisors added that Denise, at that time, did not look at "the big picture." For example, with regard to certain tasks, Denise did not know the rationale/legislative authority and more importantly, did not seem interested in knowing. This characteristic may have affected her chances in those days.

PERCEIVED FACILITATORS

Denise sees personal characteristics as key facilitators in her career progression:

- she is decisive and sticks to her decisions;
- she finishes what she takes on; and
- she has a good sense of humour.

Her colleagues confirmed this self-assessment.

Denise also considers that a good education is essential. In her day, it was not assumed that women would attend university and there was little career guidance for girls. This has changed dramatically. She took university and college continuing education courses. She found the class size in university courses intimidating, at that time. She wishes she had been more confident at age 18 and had stretched herself more.

She considers that access to training and development is important, especially for women. For example, she feels she needs computer training now.

MENTORS

Denise considers that she had several important mentors:

- The union VP, Gord, is the most important mentor. Denise really admired him and his style. She learned a great deal from him and their close working relationship. He coached her. However, she recognizes that she is not like him. He is much more "laid back" while she feels she is often very blunt, forthright.
- Lyse, the Staffing Officer, gave her opportunities to learn. Denise believes that Lyse recognized her capabilities in the CR-4 position. Her current supervisor is also very supportive but there is not the same rapport she had with Lyse.
- Mark, a former and current supervisor, has offered guidance at several stages. He notes that this is not always conscious. He sees men acting as mentors for other men more often.

ROLE MODELS

Denise's mother always worked outside the home. Her mother had to work to provide for the family as Denise's father was disabled when Denise was very young and thus unable to work outside the home. Her mother taught her to be self-reliant, "not to expect someone to take care of her." On the other hand, Denise notes a distinct absence of good role models later in life. As a result, she feels it was hard to work out paths to follow.

NETWORKING

Denise perceives networking as essential. At one point, following an in-house training session, she tried to establish an informal self-help network among administrative support staff. The idea was that they would meet over lunch and provide support and advice to each other on career matters. A senior woman in the Department offered to provide advice to the group. For some reason, it never really got off the ground.

COLLEAGUES' PERSPECTIVES

One of her mentors offered these comments on Denise's career:

Denise was the President of the largest local in National Head-quarters (NHQ) — 500 members from personnel, finance and the administration area. Gord considers this local was the most diverse and thus "hard to manage." As the President, Denise had two or three vice-presidents and a number of stewards working with (for) her. During this period, Gord was the National VP. Denise succeeded him, with his encouragement, as the National VP of the department component.

He would explain in detail his decision-making process, include her in all meetings and ask for her valued opinion. This close working rela-tionship with Denise was not fostered with the other local presidents. Denise and Gord usually talked every day regarding one issue or another. The proximity of their offices, same building but different floors, allowed this continual communication and sharing of information.

He explains that he provided this guidance unconsciously. He liked Denise, on a personal basis, and felt she was very bright and qualified and thus took an interest in working with her and providing assistance.

According to Gord, Denise's work with the union involved many different areas: planning union strategy/approach, health and safety, employment equity and any key issue that the members or manage-ment addressed. As union representatives, Gord and Denise often had to meet with very high levels of management within the Department, for example, ADM, DM. These contacts would never have occurred in their non-union positions. This level of contact has assisted them both in acquiring valuable work experience and self-confidence in dealing with superiors.

He considers that the union work provides good on-going informal training. "You learn how to deal with various types of people and situations, from upset members to hostile management. As a leader, you learn to balance the employer-employee picture. It is a skill to be able to get an employee to tell you the story without having him think you are questioning his story or taking management's side. The individual is on the defensive but you are aiming to uncover the whole situation, the real truth."

Gord notes that Denise's position in Pay and Benefits put her "at the hub of the action." If she saw a policy or procedure being ignored or changed somewhat she would let the union know. As a result, she was viewed a "royal pain in the ass" to everyone in the Department. He notes that she lacks diplomacy. Gord has told Denise that she must learn to be more diplomatic if she wants her career to progress. Her "big mouth" is advantageous in a union position and beneficial for union activity but it is not appropriate everywhere. Indeed, he advised her to keep her mouth shut.

He considers that a barrier could be her union activity. It is hard to differentiate yourself from the union once you have played such a lead role. Any identification with any specific issue can result in an individual being typecast. Gord notes people still see him as affiliated with PSAC even though his involvement was discontinued many years ago.

Having been National VP, Denise is known across the Department. This reputation is both a hindrance and a blessing in terms of career progression. He recommended to Denise that she get out of the area where people know her. It can be easier to disassociate your union involvement if you switch areas where people are not aware of your past work.

In a more general way, Gord noted that there is a stereotyping in occupational terms in the public service ("once a CR always a CR"). He does not know how this could be removed.

OTHERS

Denise's former colleagues and supervisors provided this perspective on the environment of Denise's early career:

CEIC was created, with the passage of Bill C-27 in 1977, by integrating the Unemployment Insurance Commission and the Department of Manpower and Immigration. With this amalgamation, it was decided that no one was to be declared surplus. Thus, there were too many people for the amount of work. People sat idle. Everyone tended to be territorial and guarded their jobs. During the amalgamation, careers were put on hold. Denise was not alone in encountering difficulties at this stage.

There were eventually competitions for positions within the new organization and all the staff knew there would be winners and losers. The working environment was "loose" in terms of distinguishing between the chiefs and support staff. Not everyone in the Department was comfortable given the amalgamation and unclear lines of duties. There was little distinction made between these levels which, in this individual's opinion, can lead to trouble. "It can be difficult for managers to implement decisions if they have become good friends with their staff."

A colleague from Staffing notes that there were too many PE-1s at that time and thus little room for development. She considers that Denise resented the ATs that were still brought into the Department. Generally the ATs were not well-received given the over-crowded and limited opportunities in existence. "People have to realize that new blood and bright, young, well-educated people are a benefit to the public service. In the long term their benefit far outweighs the internal promotion problems. These individuals are on training programs and often leave after it is completed."

One of Denise's former colleagues considers that CEIC did well for its employees at that time. If anyone did compete for another position elsewhere in the public service, and was successful, CEIC facilitated the move.

Another colleague noted that there are distinct organizational cultures that shape behaviours. He believed the UIC side of the Department was perceived as "efficient and people-oriented" while Manpower had a "bad reputation." He thought the UIC staff were under the impression that they would teach Manpower how to be more efficient, effective, organized, etc. His opinion was that Manpower was not accustomed to pressures, deadlines, and that the staff merely did not have the dedication that UIC staff had. "You can spot a Manpower employee a mile away even today." Denise's "roots" in Manpower may have been a disadvantage, in his opinion.

He notes that Denise's family situation also "interfered" in her early career. Denise was going through a very difficult personal crisis. "She was very cranky at work and impossible to work with." He spent many hours attempting to provide the necessary moral support, merely listening. Her private life seemed paramount. He feels she was not thinking in terms of a career. "Denise was (and is) insecure about life and herself."

Another colleague also noted that Denise was unfocused generally at that time, especially in terms of her career. This individual did not think Denise had the discipline to go after what she wanted. "Denise was of the opinion that management should do something for her." She "deserved" a good job.

Several people noted Denise was not a militant union activist but constructive. She was logical and management was able to talk to her and together they were able to reach decisions. Denise's union involvement made her more pro-people.

OTHER COMMENTS AND SUGGESTIONS

Denise and her colleagues have the following comments and suggestions:

To senior managers
- Establish real bridging positions. This may also include more rotational assignments to give support staff a chance to gain a broader perspective.
- Avoid token appointments of women. "Parachuting women into high-level jobs, which they cannot handle, is damaging to all women."
- Encourage more senior people to coach and develop their staff. This is not done and not rewarded at present.
- Training should be more than learning how to function in your present job. Further development is needed.
- Performance appraisal system must be improved. The system is there but the application is lacking. It is not a useful tool as it now stands. Everyone is "Fully Satisfactory." Results are taken with a grain of salt by managers in regards to promotion. They are "beige," saying nothing substantive.

To women
- Don't get too comfortable. Get out of the rut; be more aggressive in your own career planning. Don't be afraid to ask questions.
- Network, especially diagonally; help each other, informally. "If women are to move quicker, they must network successfully with the right people — those in power."

To men and women
- Take the time to be a mentor. At present, mentors are too rare. Many people are not willing to take that extra time and accept the added responsibility.

- People must realize their potential. "Not everyone can be stars." There is nothing wrong with being a chief, for example, enjoying one's job, doing it well and not wanting to progress any further. One may have reached their maximum work potential.
- Women and men must realize that a career requires careful planning. You must think about where you want to go in both the short term and long term. For example, people should realize that occasionally it is necessary to take a small demotion in order to transfer to a new area/department where there are opportunities for advancement in the long term.

CASE STUDY 3
Wally Clare

CURRENT SITUATION

Wally is currently the Deputy Superintendent of Bankruptcy, Consumer and Corporate Affairs (EX-1) responsible for operations and policy. He feels he is doing the best work in his career. He has made fundamental changes to the program. Despite the resource limits (135 people), he considers that the group has achieved tremendous gains. The organization was recognized by the Office of the Auditor General as one of the best in the public service.

Although he is in a senior management role, Wally keeps in touch with the clients by getting directly involved in case work from time to time. He considers this essential. His philosophy of public service emphasizes the delivery of the service to the "real people, with dignity and respect."

Wally feels the future prospects are good. "More opportunities are available." However, currently, he is satisfied with this position, feeling that he has made and continues to make a difference.

CAREER PATH

1964

Wally entered the public service directly after leaving grade 12 at age 18. He entered immediately after the end of the "hiring freeze" of the mid-1960s. There had been virtually no recruitment for several years. The thaw in staffing came with a massive recruitment campaign. Wally recalls that several thousand individuals took the entrance exams at that time. Indeed, another staff member in his area also entered the public service at that time.

Wally began working in the Patent Office as a messenger (CR-1). His duties involved bundling and mailing out patents to 17 different countries. "I was good at it. I pushed my cart faster than the next person."

You don't need so many great systems, with a great team.

Indeed, in this job, Wally set a pattern of exceeding expectations that he continued for many years.

Within a short time, Wally moved to the Print Patent Production Unit, where he had to stamp a number on each page of patent documents. There were approximately 500 patents a week, each with about 25 pages. In general, he finished this task in a day and a half. His supervisors were thus in the predicament of keeping him busy for the other three and a half days. He recalls that he sought and was given a range of other tasks and opportunities.

1965

Wally remembers that several more senior staff took an interest in both himself and his work at this stage. They involved him in interesting projects, albeit in a clerical capacity. Often these projects were demanding, but Wally learned a great deal from his involvement. Within a year of entry to the public service he was a CR-3.

1967

Within three years of entry, Wally was supervising a staff of nine people in the Patent Office Library (CR-4). This was a pivotal position for Wally. He learned a valuable lesson in supervision that formed the foundation of his subsequent management development. The Patent Library staff under his supervision included several "problem" employees. Wally thought he would "whip the unit into shape." He established a rigid set of work rules, including having staff ask for permission to leave the file room to go to the bathroom. Most of the staff worked among the stacks while Wally served the public. The staff invariably found ways of "embarrassing" him, such as asking for permission to leave the room while he was serving a client. Finally, he confronted the staff as a group. They told him he was "a pain in the ass" and that they referred to him as "little Napoleon." They told him to back off. Wally listened. He backed off and realized that he still was able to obtain results.

During this period, Wally had the opportunity of participating in a major classification exercise associated with the introduction of the current classification system. He wrote job descriptions and learned about the new system. This experience subsequently enabled him to compete for and win an AS-1 position.

1968

Wally worked in the classification area writing job descriptions. As in his messenger days, he wrote faster than the other people. Indeed, he developed techniques for work groups to collaborate in the development of a series of job descriptions. They would draft generic elements then focus on the specifics. At this stage, he began to realize that he had particular aptitudes for working with groups of people. "You have to treat people with dignity and respect. If you treat them like professionals, they act like professionals."

Wally stayed in this position approximately a year. In this time, he learned a great deal about classification and organizational issues and how they overlap. The organizational issues also inevitably spilled over into operational concerns. On several occasions, Wally was loaned to other organizations to conduct an organization/operations review.

Wally subsequently took on a series of seven or eight progressively more responsible assignments, at higher and higher occupational levels. He worked in both line and staff roles. The jobs often included a heavy "people" component. On the surface, the assignments may have had a systems label, but they generally required careful analysis of the people issues. Wally's experience reinforced earlier lessons. He recalls that he learned he could not get people to do what he wanted. "It just does not work that way. The best plans, strategies, systems and approaches fall flat without the commitment of employees." To some extent, he feels that his ego and drive to achieve got in his way at this stage. He wanted the solution to be recognizably his. "I had not really learned how to work with people and achieve recognition through their success."

1971

Wally began working for Jim, who became one of Wally's mentors, as program co-ordinator for the Corporate Bureau (AS-5). By this point, Wally had done a lot of writing in his brief career. He figured he was pretty good. One day, Jim threw him a book on basic English grammar. "He told me that some of my sentence structure would improve if I periodically used a verb." From then on, he tore apart and re-wrote everything Wally drafted. "But he required material and discussed every change he made and the reason for the change." This was devastating and frustrating. Wally thought Jim was trying to "one up" him. Finally, one day in a meeting with a number of young lawyers from Justice, Jim soundly criticized their "legalese" as being a thin disguise for an absence of content or substance. In contrast, he pointed to Wally, saying that Wally knew the substance and had learned how to write effectively. At first, Wally was angry that Jim had not provided this positive feedback earlier. In retrospect, he realized that his career would have stalled if he had not learned how to communicate effectively in writing.

1974

Wally went to Vancouver as the Regional Manager of Bankruptcy (PM-6). He took on this job as a two-year assignment with a view to learning the technical aspects of bankruptcy work. When he arrived in Vancouver, he met with the Deputy Manager, a person with long-term experience in bankruptcy. Wally offered him a deal: "I know management, you know bankruptcy. Let me teach you the management side and you teach me bankruptcy." This individual must have been at least somewhat surprised to be reporting to someone literally half his age. However, he took on the exchange. He referred to Wally as "lad" but he developed him. He did not let Wally get swamped in the very complex cases. The Deputy Manager could have set traps but he did not. When Wally left, this man became the Manager and, in the final years of his career, received a great deal of recognition.

While working on a personal bankruptcy case, Wally came face to face with the personal causes of bankruptcy. In the process of interviewing the bankrupt about the causes of the bankruptcy, he learned that the man had accidentally killed his baby while drunk, and that this symptomatic incident had contributed to his financial problems. Wally tried to proceed with the interview in the standard systematized format. "It was hopeless. I could not control the interview." That night, he cried. "The systems person in me met the people person in me." This incident raised hard questions about the system in Wally's mind. Later in his career, he has sought to address these questions.

1977

Wally returned to Ottawa a short time later. He felt a real loss in leaving. "It was the first time that I had allowed myself to be myself, without the facade of the supermanager. Working with the people I learned how to be effective without working at it." He thinks he was a very different person from the one who went to Vancouver.

Wally became the Director of Planning and Systems (SM equivalent) in a new bureau in the Department. He took a year of language training, to meet the language requirements of the position. He found language training a challenge in that he was in a class dominated by clerical employees. He felt excluded. It took a long time to get involved. Now, he fondly remembers the friends he made during that period.

The job of Director of Planning and Systems was a sharp contrast with the work he had performed in Vancouver. He was again in a staff organization. It was interesting, but he missed the day-to-day involvement with the mainline business of the bureau.

1984

Wally was appointed Deputy Superintendent of Bankruptcy (EX-1). He was again in a people-oriented role and he flourished. In reshaping the organization, Wally devoted about 15% of his budget to training and development. "You don't need so many great systems, with a great team." Wally delegated authority as far as possible down the line.

Noting that this is the longest he has spent in any job in his career, Wally commented that it also includes the most meaningful relationships. He has learned to enjoy the present. In the past, he felt he was so busy achieving and doing, he did not have time to enjoy.

Wally still keeps his hand in case work. Every year he spends a few weeks doing case work, to keep in touch with the people the program serves and their concerns.

PERCEIVED BARRIERS

Drawing from his 25-year career in the public service, Wally referred to the following barriers to the advancement of women and men:
- The lack of bridging positions can be a barrier. He noted that the AS-1 position he occupied was such a bridge. Wally has deliberately created eight bridging positions in his organization, offering the same training as offered to the external recruits.
- Specialized educational or experience requirements can effectively screen women out of competitions. It becomes a convenient excuse that "no qualified women are available." Wally's own response to this is to create an internal training program: four months of intensive classroom training in enforcement and in bankruptcy practices. "The first wave may reach the PM-6 level this year."
- Not all managers are willing or able to be mentors. Many are too insecure. A colleague of Wally's recalled that she did not actively assume the role of a mentor although other staff attributed the role to her. She did assist women if they came to her with concerns or questions. She would always relay her experiences. She feels that mentoring takes a lot of work and is a big responsibility, thus she did not assume the role.

WORK ENVIRONMENT

In the past, the official receivers (ORs) were ex-RCMP, ex-military, ex-policemen and consequently the role was viewed as being enforcement. Men definitely used to dominate the branch. One female manager explained that she is not a confrontational woman and that she did not enjoy the treatment she received over the years. "I dislike confrontations and grew tired of the comments, insinuations, etc." As more women entered the branch this individual was always willing to listen to the newer women and to help them understand that they were not the only ones encountering these situations.

It was interesting that these ORs do not view themselves as civil servants because they deal primarily with the external environment in the course of their work. They believe they have acquired the respect from the external environment; that is, trustees, creditors, community — bankrupts. Their job encompasses "the best of both worlds" according to these colleagues.

A "team work" approach is present throughout the branch. The ORs described their working days as interesting and diverse in scope and nature.

BALANCING FAMILY AND CAREER

Balance is very important to Wally. He has an active volunteer life, working in the area of drug and alcohol addiction. He and his wife work together in giving a program for couples who have been affected by alcohol and drugs in their family. This volunteer commitment has evolved over the years. Wally is Chairman of the Board and President of Serenity Renewal for Families, which has a client base of 8,500 people including many from all parts of Canada.

Wally's colleagues agreed that it was crucial to be able to balance a family and a career effectively. Their individual circumstances are described below.

Vivian was a single parent of three, and worked two nights a week cleaning houses in addition to her full-time position in Consumer Services.

Heather's husband is very supportive of her career and shares the family and household responsibilities. If this was not the case, Heather could not do the work of an OR. When Heather was a single parent, she was very careful not to be absent from work for family responsibility reasons. She supervised clerical staff at that time and was proud to state that her attendance record was better than all her staff.

Sylvie notes she is away on business a fair amount. She views this absence as a positive factor in her children's relationship with their father. For example, the children, at first, cried that only Mom made them breakfast, not Dad. However, once the children realized that Mom was away, Dad took over some of the duties that the children used to allow only Mom to do. The father-child relationship grew, in Sylvie's opinion. Sylvie also related her father's strong belief that women belong at home with the children. When she was expecting her first child, her father's comment was "now you will quit your job." Sylvie replied that no, she would not quit her job because she was having a baby. When Sylvie became pregnant with their second child, her father again said that now she would have to quit her job. Sylvie replied that no, she was not going to quit because she was having a second child.

All three agreed that women still perform the majority of family responsibilities. Although more spouses are assisting, the overall responsibility lies with the wife.

PERCEIVED FACILITATORS
On the other side of the coin, Wally's comments regarding facilitators in career advancement were:
- He regards the diversity of his work experience and his experience with many different managers as being particularly valuable.
- Wally considers that being able to assess oneself honestly and accurately is essential. In contrast, he feels that most people in the public service are more concerned with image and other people's views.
- He finds that the women are very energetic and committed. Currently, he is running a competition for a senior position and expects that women candidates will perform very well. "The reality is that many women still think and work as though they have to be 25% better" in order to be on an equal footing with the man doing the same job.

SELF-ASSESSMENT
Looking back, Wally made the following candid remarks regarding his strengths and weaknesses:
- He regards his ego as a liability in his early years, although, fortunately, not a heavy liability. "It is a liability of most managers that they need to demonstrate that they have the answers. They don't unlock the capacity of staff." In the same vein, he noted that five or ten years ago, he would have wanted his own contribution to the Auditor General's award to be visible. He has learned to share recognition with 135 people.

- Wally considers his ability to work with people and to develop their commitment as a major asset. Ottawa is a "town of systems people," who forget what the systems are supposed to do. Despite his people orientation, Wally has implemented major systems in the bureau. "We have to be good, slick managers, not for our sake, but so that we can humour the system and free ourselves to do a good job."
- "I prided myself on making hard, effective decisions and insisted on the right to make decisions. Now I don't need to. The staff make the decisions. I affirm or support them. This gives me the ultimate in authority, their commitment."
- Wally considers he was very goal-oriented. In retrospect, he considers that the first ten years of his career were "very punishing" years. He had a drive to succeed and threw everything into it. He feels he missed enjoying the current situation because he always focused on the future. Today, he seeks more balance as quoted earlier.

MENTORS

Wally credits some of his success to the mentors he had:
- Jim, particularly for the development of writing skills and setting standards for planning and evaluating results.
- A former Superintendent of Bankruptcy encouraged Wally to get field experience that was essential for further development. He also showed Wally the need to enjoy life, to have fun in your work and to make the job fun for the people who work for you.
- A male manager, very early in Wally's career, stressed the need to have management values and to assert what you believe in. "Healthy managers have healthy disagreement systems. Because we disagree on a particular issue does not mean we don't like or respect each other. We disagree and that is both healthy and okay in an open organization."

ROLE MODELS

This issue was discussed with the colleagues, who made the following statements:
- Vivian's mother was her role model, although she knew she could never live up to her mother's standards. Her mother was a physician with six children, involved with volunteer work and a very strong, dynamic woman. Her mother was unbelievable — a real "superwoman" before her time.

- Sylvie was one of the first women in many of her positions within Bankruptcy. She did not have a role model within the branch. She did, however, read many women's biographies that she was able to learn from and that made her feel she was not the only one in the world facing male confrontation.
- Vivian and Heather commented that Sylvie was somewhat of a model (inspiration) to them when they first entered the branch.

ROLE OF INDIVIDUAL MANAGERS

In five years, Wally has increased the proportion of women in officer roles from less than 10% to roughly 50%. He did it with a variety of recruitment and development techniques including: formal training and development programs, bridging positions and university recruitment. He consciously did not simply bring in two women managers, which would have satisfied the "target" he had been given. Instead, he began to build a balanced organization, bringing women in at the working level using the above techniques.

He recalls that the men in the organization were upset initially, calling his actions "reverse discrimination." Wally acknowledged that it was a strong affirmative action program and the goal was a balanced organization that could deliver services more effectively. The men seem to have adjusted. A few still may consider it "demeaning" to work for a woman.

At a recent conference of all the case officers, Wally was moved to notice the balance of men and women in the room.

Three women official receivers, who work with Wally, spoke highly of the training and development offered through the branch. Heather's and Sylvie's intensive OR training was viewed positively.

On-going training is also evident; for example, they recently attended a conference concerning gambling and its causes and consequences. In terms of Wally's efforts in Bankruptcy (the hiring and training of women as official receivers), these colleagues remarked that it sets an example for other departments that it can be done. They were very positive towards Wally and his efforts regarding the advancement of women. They called him a "visionary," an "exciting man" and a "future-oriented" individual. Vivian commented that Wally is very supportive of women, "he genuinely likes women, probably more so than men in terms of work relationships." She also commented that he does not feel threatened by women and, in her opinion, his actions are due in part to his healthy relationship with his wife.

They recalled Wally's idea for a retreat of all female non-clerical staff at Gray Rocks. It was exceptional. Sylvie attended this retreat. She felt it was very effective in terms of networking and finding out other women had similar concerns/problems. Everyone returned to work after having learned something about themselves, men and women in general and the branch. The network foundation was put into place.

Apparently, some of the men who were the most negative are now the most proactive supporters of women in the branch. They believe the system itself has improved with the introduction of women. Sylvie and Heather commented that they, as women, were initially fearful in bringing women into Bankruptcy in such droves. They were afraid that if the situation was not handled properly, it could harm all the women.

OTHER COMMENTS AND SUGGESTIONS

Wally and his colleagues also made a number of other comments and suggestions:

- "Work on the women first" — often women have a self-defeating attitude that must be adjusted. For example, Sylvie never assumed she could do a job of a higher classification. Someone had to ask her why she was not entering a competition, "hold her hand."
- Women must receive an equal chance for advancement. Bridging and acting positions are a good vehicle for advancement.
- Quotas do not work. A systems solution will not work. Managers are very adept at side-stepping systems to get what they want. Somehow, managers must develop a commitment to change. "A good manager can walk around the system, but one committed manager will do more than all the systems."
- Often the system designers are the "controllers" of the world. They need to put into place all kinds of controls to ensure things are done their way and inevitably it is the excessive controls and monitoring that defeat the initiative.
- There is a need to convince many managers that the benefit of a balanced organization is a better, more meaningful and responsive public service.
- The development of better opportunities for women in the public service is too important to be left exclusively to women managers. There is a need to involve men in all aspects and at all levels of the initiatives taken.

- Important to support women once they are placed in a "token" position/place. Women cannot succeed in a position without a support network. Do not promote a woman into a high position and then forget about her.
- "Parachuting" women into high positions does not work.
- There is less resentment with bringing women up the ranks, providing them with the necessary training to advance, letting them prove themselves not only to others but also to themselves.
- There should be more part-time opportunities within the public service. A person should not be treated as any less of an employee simply because they work part-time and not full-time.
- Lack of day-care facilities provided by the public service. In comparison to other large organizations, the current public service situation is a disgrace.
- Vivian was adamant that people must recognize that changes to improve the advancement opportunities for women cannot be legislated. It is a change of attitudes that must occur.

CASE STUDY 4
Joanne Martin

When I would

suggest asking

about industry

views, I was

seen as

a moron.

CURRENT SITUATION

Since the fall of 1986, Joanne has been the manager (SM) of a division in Industry, Science and Technology that includes responsibility for a highly traditional male-dominated industry sector currently in trouble. The position focuses on a sector that involves extensive industry inter-action. Since the industry is predominantly located in economically depressed regions, there is a strong industrial and regional develop-ment flavour to the role. The position also includes responsibilities for an emerging industry sector, ocean industries (for example, the Hibernia off-shore oil and gas development), marine equipment and pleasure craft.

It is a very politically sensitive and high-profile area. Any problems in the industry are quickly reflected on page one of the papers and result in questions in the House. There is frequent communication to the political level, with Cabinet documents and briefings. Joanne has an approximate $70 million annual budget under vote 10 and $200,000-$300,000 O&M budget.

Joanne reflects "the pressure of the position can take its toll."

CAREER PATH

1974

Joanne joined the public service directly out of university where she had completed an honours degree in economics. Joanne had worked with DREE as a summer student in 1973 and enjoyed it. She applied for the Administrative Trainee Program, thinking that she would stay only a few years with the public service.

Her first position was in Transport Canada in the area of urban and regional transportation policy as an Administrative Trainee. At that time, the idea was that new recruits stayed at the Administrative

Trainee level for about 18 months. Her supervisor had also recently joined the public service from the private sector. He quickly recognized her skills and offered her an ES-1 position, doing the same work within the policy group.

1975

The demise of the federal urban affairs department and changes in government priorities resulted in a declining involvement in urban and regional transportation issues on the part of Transport Canada. A number of staff within the policy group were reassigned to focus on energy in transportation. The energy issue had really begun to develop at this point. Joanne had her first wide exposure in working with industry at this stage and found it very interesting (ES-5).

During this period, she also organized the Transport Canada in-house energy conservation program. This experience provided her with excellent exposure to administration across the Department. It also helped her to recognize that she preferred a policy role to an administrative role.

1977

Eventually, "the glow wore off" on the energy issue. The policy group was reorganized to an issues oriented "hit squad" of policy developers. Among other projects, Joanne was assigned to work on the Polar 10 Icebreaker project, focusing on the industrial benefits that would accrue from the project (ES-5).

1978

By this point, Joanne thought that she had been in Transport Canada a long time and was beginning to look for something different. A person with whom she had worked in Transport Canada, who was now working in the small business development area, suggested that she transfer over to Industry, Trade and Commerce. She did so, largely to pursue "something new." The work again involved considerable industry interface, albeit with a more entrepreneurial sector.

During this period, she was also responsible for representing the branch and the Department on affirmative action issues vis-à-vis the Status of Women "Employment Action for Women" program and the internal affirmative action program. She considers the credibility she achieved for this program within ITC as one of her significant successes.

The opportunity of a promotion was held out, but never materialized. By this time she had completed an MBA program on a part-time basis at the University of Ottawa. When the reorganization from ITC to DRIE began, Joanne realized that she would have to move out to move up. She saw a newspaper advertisement for a CO-3 position in EMR, in the area of Canadian ownership and control determination of companies in the oil and gas sector.

1982

Joanne responded to the advertisement because of an interest in the energy area and was invited for an interview. She recalls that her interview was at 4 p.m. It was a very "staid" board. She did not think she had much of a chance since she had little technical exposure to the energy sector. However, the nature of the questions was very analytical and she quickly relaxed and enjoyed the interview. She was offered the job.

It was a growth period for the energy sector at EMR. Many young, aggressive people entered the Department at the same time. Management, on the other hand, was older and more traditional. Joanne again was involved in extensive industry interaction. She analyzed the ownership structures of large firms involved in the oil and gas sector, focusing on questions such as who the beneficial owners were, where control lay and financial stability.

In the process of gearing up for the COR/CS (Canadian Ownership and Control Determination) program, Joanne did the final bilingual imperative staffing and ran the Calgary office for a period. When this was complete, she did not feel like going back to reviewing applications and the auditing process, which was about to begin, held no appeal for Joanne. She looked for something else. EMR did not seem to offer much opportunity. She contends that it was very hard for someone who was not a geologist or engineer to find a place in that department, even though the technical specialists often lacked the experience and skills for industry interface.

In all, she had spent about 18 months in EMR. "I was one of the first in and first out" Joanne explained in reference to the Petroleum Incentives Administration. "There was nowhere to go in EMR." Joanne firmly considers that one of the weaknesses of the technical departments is generally their poor understanding of industry and the economy as a whole. Yet her skills in this area were largely seen as expendable. "When I would suggest asking about industry views, I was seen as a moron."

One of Joanne's colleagues from EMR, who also entered the Department (at a management level) during the early 1980s, agreed with Joanne's assessment of the opportunities in that department. Indeed, she bluntly commented "A woman with a career in EMR, that's a contradiction in terms." She feels that the Department's downsizing has had a disproportionate effect on women.

1983

A former colleague from the small business group at ITC, who had become a manager in the food area of DRIE during the reorganization, contacted her and explained that he was looking for a policy person to do government-industry relations and strategic planning. It "sounded like fun" and she pursued the opportunity. She was interviewed by the Director General, who asked her about her experience with the food industry. Joanne explained that apart from eating and shopping "when she couldn't delegate" she had little knowledge of the industry but that she had broad experience in dealing with the industry-government interface.

Joanne spent a very interesting and stimulating two years in this area. Her skills in understanding corporate structures assisted her in analyzing the intricate ownership structures of firms like Labatts. It was a busy period. She was travelling about three weeks out of four.

In the fall of 1984, the issue of industrial applications of biotechnology began to surface, first in the food area. Joanne was asked to write a Cabinet discussion paper. To do so, she set up a task force, involving the regional offices of the Department. She travelled to each region to consult with people and returned to write up the paper. She is proud that she wrote it in one draft then revised it. It went forward from there. This paper "put biotechnology on the map for the Department."

Shortly afterwards she became pregnant and began to plan for maternity leave. When her daughter was born, Joanne took two months maternity leave and worked at home for a third month.

1985

Upon her return from maternity leave, she was again the acting manager, first while her supervisor was on a major trip and then while he was ill. She enjoyed the excitement of the biotechnology issue development but was frustrated in the acting role: "responsibility but no authority." At the same time, it was a good opportunity to learn the management ropes. During this period, the biotechnology issue "really moved." Joanne was involved in setting up an association. She began to realize, however, that the food group at DRIE would not ultimately have responsibility for the development of the technology area. She did not see long-term prospects that the excitement would continue.

In the summer of 1986, as she was on her way out the door to a bio-technology conference in Quebec City, Joanne received a call from the PSC inviting her to compete for an SM position in the marine group. She did not have much time to talk but asked that the background material be sent over. It seemed to be a long jump from food to shipbuilding. However, it also seemed very familiar, due to her experience in Transport Canada and her broad experience with government-industry interaction.

Joanne let her name stand. She figured she did not have much chance as someone had been acting in the position. The interview was on a Friday afternoon. Fortunately, the interview style was "thinking" rather than "detailed nuts and bolts knowledge." The discussion in the interview ranged over socio-economic and policy implications of the industry. It was a "fun" interview, not a strict examination.

Joanne received a call first thing on Monday. The Director of the group asked whether she could "assume" Joanne was still interested in the position. Joanne was offered the job but she had some reservations about accepting it. She felt that she was abandoning the other job. The manager for whom she was acting was still ill, but expected to return. She knew that she could not "go back" to an officer role. She deliberated carefully over the decision. She felt that the manager was a good friend and she did not want to let him down.

1986

In the fall of 1986, Joanne assumed her current position. She had a tremendous déjà vu feeling at first. She interacted with many of the same people she had worked with at Transport Canada ten years earlier. On the Polar Icebreaker project, the main difference was that in the 1970s the focus had been on a state of the art icebreaker, the nuclear-powered Polar 10. That concept had been scaled down to a more mundane conventionally-powered Polar 8. Joanne's focus was again on the industrial development side of the marine world.

FUTURE PROSPECTS

Joanne feels that the path ahead simply is not clear. She had, however, been contacted by a person at the ADM level in DND, who frequently offered advice to people on career advancement possibilities. He commented that her career path appears erratic. "What does this woman want to do?" Joanne realized that she had to make the pattern more visible.

Joanne is currently looking for an EX-2 position but feels she will probably have to settle for an EX-1, at least in the interim. She recently had an opportunity to transfer to three different areas, one of which had always fascinated her. In that instance, the possibility was raised of replacing the director general when he moved on. However, Joanne decided that the position was effectively a demotion, the budget was smaller and the position was less visible.

The high tech area, with its innovation and entrepreneurial approaches, appeals to her. "I am biding my time right now. I am comfortable here and I like the marine subject area. I have good credibility. Marine is not considered a lightweight, fluffy industry."

TURNING POINTS
Looking back, Joanne saw a number of turning points in her career:
- early opportunity to enter the ES group from her AT position;
- acting as manager in the food division during the initiation of a major new policy thrust, biotechnology policy; and
- her drive to do work that interests and stimulates her, "It had to be interesting. You have to enjoy what you do."

Joanne acknowledges that she did not plan her career, at least in the early years. It evolved. Looking back on her career, Joanne notes that it does appear somewhat erratic. However, she feels there is a clear pattern at the functional rather than the subject level with strong industry-government and policy involvement in different subject areas.

PERCEIVED BARRIERS
From Joanne's perspective, the following are barriers that confront men and women in the public service:
- Joanne sees the main barrier as a demographic/structural one. There are fewer and fewer opportunities for advancement with a lot of people in their thirties and forties interested in the positions.
- Downsizing and staffing from surplus lists further reduces opportunities.
- The old boys' network is still very much alive, especially in the "harder," more technical divisions and departments. For example, there appears to be a network among Transport Canada, Fisheries and Oceans and DRIE/IST in the marine area.

- The culture of an organization can pose a barrier to outsiders, including women. EMR is one of the hard-core technical departments. Traditionally, there have been fewer women with the specialized expertise employed in EMR. However, Joanne wonders whether specialized technical background is really an asset or rather an artificial and unnecessary requirement for many positions. The age factor is also important. Departments like EMR were staffed in the 1950s and 1960s, when there were fewer women in the labour force. On the other hand, they had their chance to open up. The National Energy Program brought in a lot of top-notch women: economists, lawyers and accountants. They did not stay. They were never really integrated into the Department. She contends that the entire program was seen as peripheral, a "whim of the politicians."

A former colleague of Joanne's remarked that the socialized differences in men and women are very "powerful." She believes this socialization is a form of a barrier that makes the sexes act and think very differently. She personally does not want to change or acquire male characteristics in order to progress in her career.

This same individual agreed with Joanne in terms of the demographic/structural barrier. She finds there is no room for advancement in her current department. Her experience has also led her to conclude that lateral transfers do not always provide the career recognition one would hope.

A colleague of Joanne's with many years of experience in Transport Canada mentioned that the Department often brings in people from the outside to fill higher level positions. This is very "disappointing and annoying" for those, both male and female, in the Department awaiting such a vacant job opportunity. "We often find out a position is filled when the individual shows up at the desk on a Monday morning." In connection to the above, she remarked that career planning is non-existent in the Department, from her experience. Each individual must assume this task alone.

BALANCING FAMILY AND CAREER

While balancing her career and family responsibilities takes a lot of energy, Joanne feels that there is a compensating set of rewards.

Joanne has a full-time nanny. Until her daughter was 18 months old, her mother-in-law stayed with the family. Part of the challenge in balancing her career and family is that Joanne really enjoys her daughter's company. "I try not to take work home, but I cannot always avoid it. Things like appraisals and work plans almost invariably have to be done at home, in the evening or on weekends or holidays."

A colleague of Joanne's remarked that women are still the primary care-givers in terms of a family. The majority of the responsibility rests with the woman. She could not think of a couple where the man assumed at least half the family responsibilities and duties.

Another colleague mentioned that it was interesting that all the women in her department in upper management did not have children.

One of Joanne's former colleagues expressed great admiration for Joanne's capacity to handle diverse demands so effectively. She considered Joanne a truly exceptional person "Did she tell you she was trilingual? She learned German after she got her MBA."

PERCEIVED FACILITATORS

Joanne was adamant that hard work and the willingness to go the distance are critical success factors for career progression. Joanne recalled her farm background and the fact that she learned independence and self-reliance at a very early age. She was always involved in farm work, out of economic necessity. Joanne remembers driving the tractor when she was not yet strong enough to steer it around the corners.

Joanne was the second of four children and considers that she was somewhat "invisible." She always tried to earn her father's respect. It made her a "closet perfectionist." She learned to be extremely conscientious and time sensitive.

SELF-ASSESSMENT

Joanne attributes much of her success to the following strengths:
- breadth of knowledge: "I read widely and think widely";
- broad exposure to industry-government relations;
- extensive understanding of industrial and corporate strategies and cultures, she sees both similarities and distinctions across industries, — "Patterns recur";
- very good writing and analytical skills;
- strong oral communication skills;
- good delegation skills: "I encourage independence in my staff. I am not going to tell anyone how to suck eggs"; and
- team style.

A colleague remarked that Joanne was a good example of an "ambitious and career-minded individual."

MENTORS

Joanne does not like this concept. On the other hand, she feels it is always important to work for a supervisor you respect. This has always been a factor for her in looking at career options. Joanne considers it very important to seek out managers whose skills she respects and from whom she can learn.

One colleague, who had a negative experience with a mentor, explained that she may never be "real enough and trust enough" to find a mentor again. She is not sure if she would "risk it again." However, she has helped some of her staff. For example, she assisted one male staff member to overcome a racial barrier. This individual is progressing well and she is very pleased and excited for him.

Another colleague, who had never experienced a mentoring relationship, pointed out there are good and bad mentoring relationships. She remarked that the individual should ensure that the person they are promoting is qualified for the career progression. She has seen instances whereby an unqualified individual received promotions based merely on "who he knew and who had taken him under his wing." This individual's promotion had a negative effect on morale in the Department.

ROLE MODELS

Joanne considers that she had virtually no role models when she was young. She tries to offer a role model to others.

COLLEAGUES' PERSPECTIVES

Diane, a former colleague of Joanne's who entered the public service around the same time and is now also a manager, was candid in describing the environment in her area of a large technical department. This individual spent approximately four years in a particular area that she described as "male chauvinistic to the extreme." At that time, mid-70s, Diane recalled that this department was dominated by "ex-military" male personnel who had an "authoritarian view of the world."

Diane entered this department as an Administrative Trainee with relatively little work experience but a formal university education. She began to work for a male director who provided her with valuable work experience and "I accepted him as my mentor." He was quite helpful in the initial stages of their work relationship. Unfortunately, he eventually "propositioned" her and when she refused he began to "make my life hell." She recalls being very naive at the time. She was unaware that she could approach the union and she was disappointed with the reception she received in Personnel when she explained her situation. Personnel's reaction was basically "tough." This treatment from her director continued and Diane acquired bleeding ulcers. She remembers feeling "how could this be happening to me?" She was shocked and felt she had no one to talk to. She became the "black sheep" of the group and no one would associate with her. In effect, her director ostracized her. She recalls the day she received a new position outside of the Department, "I hung up the phone after receiving the job offer and shouted ecstatically "I'm free." Her director never said good-bye to her when she left.

Diane also described the "ageism" that was apparent in promotions. She remembers being told she was "too young to be classified as a PM-5." Her position, at the time, was a PM-3 and classification audits of her position gave results of a PM-5 level; however, her director was determined to keep the position at only a PM-3. He was successful in this regard.

Another situation Diane described involved a project she was co-ordinating. A number of people were responsible for providing her with sections of the project. One individual, a male, "patted me on the head and said he was not ready to give it to me." This individual told her boss to "get your Girl Friday off my back."

In conclusion, Diane explained that in the mid-70s the women in the Department were generally young and inexperienced. They were identifiable and easily differentiated from the rest of the staff. In contrast, the young men in the same situation tended to fit better into the environment, its culture and its characteristics.

A colleague also remarked that her opinion is one of "diminishing returns" when it comes to women working extremely hard in order to succeed. From her experience, she has seen many women burn out far more quickly than their career progresses.

Another one of Joanne's colleagues, currently an EX-1, agreed with that assessment. Although she has invested long hours in her career, she is now considering options outside the public service.

OTHER COMMENTS AND SUGGESTIONS

Joanne and her colleagues had the following recommendations:
- Women must have stamina and remain cool and professional in all their business matters. Women must find problem-solving routes that are professional in nature.

- System will not deal with people who are not team players.
- System must "treat people as people and work as work."
- Women must "appear to be on the inside."
- Men must not continue to regard women as threats but rather as healthy and worthwhile competitors.
- Both men and women must look out for themselves. Career planning and progression "is up to you personally. Departments are passive, vacancies often not advertised and personnel often plays an inactive role."
- Base promotions on the candidates' qualifications and experience and not on who they know.

SELECTED COMMENTS

PROVIDED BY
RESPONDENTS
TO QUESTION 47

I would first like to say thank you for asking my opinion. I hope my comments, along with those of the other respondents, will provide some hints as to how to eliminate these barriers to advancement.

Advancement in the public service (once on permanent status) is primarily through competition and appointment without competition. The competition process is very often lengthy and time consuming, so personnel staff will often fill a position through exclusion order rather than go through the whole procedure. I believe there are vacancies to which I could advance but which are being filled by persons hired under the exclusion orders. I suspect also that a great number of competitions are open only to indeterminate employees within a particular department. I am not permitted to compete with another CR-3 government employee even though we both work for the same employer. It appears to me that the competition/ transfer/appointment system could do with a bit of revamping in order to encourage people to move up.

Training — In my office we are expected to train ourselves, beyond the first introduction to the system. Being shortstaffed, training beyond the point of "enough to be productive" is not provided. (For example: a new computer program is brought on-line, a manual is printed out and everyone is expected to learn it in a week.) It takes a longer time to learn on your own and sometimes critical points are missed. This is not "developmental" training, but if people cannot handle a program they have been working with for a year, and their Personal Evaluation Report (appraisal) reflects this, the opportunity for advancement through competition is diminished by their rating.

A more rigidly enforced training system might ensure that each individual becomes competent enough to advance. The biggest reason is lack of training funds. I believe that the return on training funds investment is high enough to make it worthwhile.

Classification — Why is the CR group only split into seven levels? Duties of a CR vary considerably. All office-type work is not the same, especially since the installation of computers. My job description rating is already at the top of the CR knowledge scale and I am only a CR-03. I am now doing work which in the private sector is being paid $6,000 - $8,000 more annually. The private sector can fluctuate, but the CR rating scale has not been modified to reflect changing technology and new work procedures. Getting the classification rating for my position changed has been an inter-sectional nightmare lasting since before I took over the job. There is also no standardization across the

I believe that the return on training funds investment is high enough to make it worthwhile.

country, let alone equal pay for work of equal value. My current classification rating prevents me from being recognized for what work I really do, especially when being considered during competitions (for example: "She's only a CR-03 and she is going for an AS-1 position?"). I would like to add that I have never found advancement limitations based on the fact that I am a woman. I have found "the system" more inhospitable than the people.

Managers should not be allowed to refuse a person's request for the advancement courses they desire. In my field I just slide back down a hill because I'm not being kept up-to-date! Yet the men get the courses!

• • • • •

In my particular situation, my male supervisor knows that I am necessary to the operation as I am told I am "the brightest, the smartest, the one with the most experience." However, this is only when problems arise and I am therefore the only one to "fix them." The rest of the time I am ignored and not included in any office matters. There is another female co-worker who experiences the same type of harassment.

As I am an active member of our union, I find that management will hold this against you whether you are male or female and label you as a "disturber."

I find that management feels threatened or is insecure with employees who show initiative, who are intelligent and ask management "Why?". Management is much happier with employees who agree with them and do not question; I would like to think that workers should not have to behave like sheep to work comfortably in their jobs.

The social barriers that have been established for years still must be overcome. These include — women can only do the typical "women's jobs" and certainly can't do a man's job; that men are supervisors and managers because they are smarter — these must still be overcome before we have a compatible working situation.

• • • • •

I would like to see more training courses offered, and not be denied training because of operational requirements. Some areas in our department receive all training being offered, but I have often been denied, or not been told of training courses being offered simply because the workplace could not afford to let me go.

• • • • •

In the past, I have applied on internal competitions for other categories, in particular finance and administration (FI-1/FI-2). There's never a problem qualifying from an educational standpoint, having an accounting designation, but I'm always screened out for lack of experience. I'm not saying there aren't more experienced individuals, especially those working in the area, but what I resent is the fact that:

(i) I don't even get an interview.

(ii) Although I may lack "specific" experience in relation to the position, as an auditor I work in the business community and have experience and training in accounting and finance.

(iii) The knowledge and experience required in my position is easily comparable to the competition applied for (FI-01/02) but this does not appear to be taken into consideration at the initial screening of applicants.

・・・・・

First of all I strongly disagree with this visible minority stuff. A person should be hired according to their education and capability of handling the job. Secondly I feel literature should be passed out amongst federal servants for job postings, i.e., what the job details are. As well there could be special "federal" courses that a federal employee could enrol in for future advancement or for better inter-office skills.

・・・・・

I think the practice of appointing persons from outside the federal public service is a barrier to all men and women already in the public service. This has already occurred in my own office. An outsider has been appointed to a PM-2 level on a six-month term which will probably go up for competition after this period. I feel it is most unfair as there are probably plenty of PM-1s and possibly PM-2s who would have loved the opportunity which is denied to them. The particular PM-2 position was created for the lucky person. The qualifications of this person are by no means out of the ordinary and I feel that the same work experiences may be shared by many already in the public service seeking a promotion or transfer.

・・・・・

Basically, I feel employment opportunities in the public service are fair, albeit not always in some circumstances. The term "Government of Canada is an Equal Opportunity Employer" brings out giggles of mirth at times. However, not to belabour the public service, I truly believe it tries hard, and it should be noted that there will always be instances whereby a competition was not run by the rules, or will not be run in accordance with scrupulous fairness. The trick is to see the unfairness before it happens or after a competition has been conducted, nullify the results if any anomalies appear. However, do so more swiftly, don't lag or hold back, as has happened in the past. All that happens is you get disgruntled, discontented competitors.

In regards to women not being considered for promotion, this is one area that the Government has made great strides. In the department I work in, the top public servant has been a women for the past 35 years, until recently when a male won the last competition. As a male, I do see sexist behaviour towards women; at one time it was outwardly stated, where now, because of a new set of watchdogs, it is done deceptively, ever so subtly most times.

When referring to visible minorities, or the disabled being left behind in the promotional arena — I can't speak or write with any authority regarding the disabled, but I have worked closely with three people who are considered to be a part of the visible minority sector. When a form asking people who are members of a visible minority to identify themselves was circulated, it set off a set of mixed reactions. All three on first look at the form considered it to be downright insulting, and on second and third look had not changed their opinions.

· · · · ·

I am employed in DND as a technician repairing electrical, mechanical, and optical instruments. Barriers to advancement I feel are in the lack of specialized training — technical courses related to the trade that are not available to the civilian work force.

· · · · ·

I feel that the competition process in the public service can be a barrier to advancement. Some of the questions asked are so detailed that one can't adequately provide the answer unless the person is already working in the position. Also, some of the personnel sections of certain departments are not very helpful in providing information regarding the position and the department itself. As well, I feel that I'm stuck in the middle at times when applying for officer-level positions. For example, when I graduated from university, I was told that I didn't have the required experience for the officer-level jobs. Now that I have acquired some work experience I have lost most of my post-secondary knowledge due to lack of application on the job. I feel sometimes that I am always one step behind, either lacking experience or knowledge. However, I am neither discouraged nor upset because I believe in myself and my ability and I know that eventually I will be promoted to a higher position due to sheer hard work. I want to make a difference as a public servant and I'm doing just that everyday, no matter what position I'm in.

· · · · ·

Other people are constantly being treated unfairly and not given opportunities. File a grievance and watch your opportunities go down the tube. Speak out or disagree with management and you are labelled a rebel/radical/troublemaker.

· · · · ·

Restyle the competition system. Give more consideration to employees with longer-term, satisfactory work records and assessments. Sometimes younger, short-term employees have the advantage when it comes to written competitions, but they do not understand the running of the department and they do not have the work experience or the leadership ability required for the position.

Quite often the training of this inexperienced employee falls back on the more experienced employee who was at a disadvantage because of a written competition. This situation does not serve the department well.

A common complaint in the public service is the shortage of developmental opportunities, such as associated trade courses, and for those employees with the desire and the aptitude, administration courses — stats reporting, supply procedures, etc. Many times, due to changes in management personnel, employees find themselves in a position for which they are not prepared.

Sometimes managers and supervisors are backwards about imparting their knowledge and information to subordinates — I assume they don't want their subordinates to be as knowledgeable as they are. This reflects a lack of confidence and may create a lack of trust in subordinates. This is not good enough.

Employees that are kept well informed are better able to understand unusual situations and requests when they arise. This leads to better labour/management relations and therefore leads to the job getting done better and more efficiently.

· · · · ·

I believe that although it may be more difficult for women to obtain positions and advancement in non-traditional occupations, the affirmative action program hires or promotes candidates that are not as qualified as their male counterparts. This promotes resentment in the workplace against women in these positions, and is self-defeating as some of the people hired simply cannot do the job. All candidates should be hired solely on their merit.

· · · · ·

I have worked for both the RCMP and Employment and Immigration in a clerical capacity, and after a total of eight years in the public service, it is apparent that it is much easier to advance in certain departments.

For example, in the RCMP, a public servant can only advance if he/she is willing to work in an urban area or regional HQ.

Further, in the RCMP, men, predictably, occupy most of the management positions which, in some cases, costs taxpayers a lot more than I feel is necessary. For example, at HQ, women could be handling much of the workload that is assigned to constables who are fresh out of depot division.

. . . . .

Personal life styles should be kept out of advancement, i.e., golfing with the right people, associating with the "right group."

Reasons for advancement should not be that you've sobered up and joined AA or that you're in a minority group. It should be that you've proven yourself to be capable and responsible on the job and have conducted yourself in a professional manner.

Since Correctional Services Canada (CSC) is a human endeavour, staff should not be held back because of lack of education. Many people who did not complete grade 12 or university have the ability to work with others and are very capable people. They have got years of experience in dealing with a wide range of people and have a wide scope in job related functions. Through raising families and dealing with the work force and being involved in community work they have a lot to offer CSC. Younger staff may have the book knowledge but no common sense. I think a cross section of each would be a better balance. Offenders often seek out the more reliable, older staff rather than the educated younger staff because they feel more comfortable with them. They can relate to someone who has had several jobs and raised a family and can deal with them in a "common sense way." If they try to force them into a book mold the relationship will fail.

I've usually found younger staff have all kinds of theories about offenders when they come in, but know very little about human nature!

. . . . .

The "merit principle" is not followed in a substantial number of competitions (particularly at the senior levels).

There is too much emphasis on "quotas" rather than staffing based on qualifications.

Performance appraisals and work references should have much more importance in staffing.

How many people are really bilingual? This applies to both English-speaking and French-speaking people. Is the money spent on language training being wasted?

· · · · ·

I believe that people should be hired according to their skills, experience and past performance and not because they are women or a visible minority. It has become a major disadvantage to be a unilingual English white male. That's not fair.

· · · · ·

I am in the management category in the Government. I am also in a specialized technical field. Being a women I now have three major strikes against being promoted — in spite of the fact that I get superior appraisals and am bilingual to level B. The SM/EX levels of this department are 85-90% male. The informatics field is 99.9% male, the management completely male. Men at senior levels hire men and are reluctant to hire women managers. Women who act like men are more likely to get promotions.

· · · · ·

It seems in our department when someone is interested in a certain area, management seems to make sure you don't go near that area. Instead of putting them in areas they like, they put them in areas they hate or do not like very much, giving the workers low morale, which is a very bad problem in the public service.

· · · · ·

Language training should be more easily accessible as it is a prerequisite to promotion in most government offices.

· · · · ·

Who you know is important — some people naturally get along better with people and know how to multiply their contacts. Others may have lots of abilities and knowledge but don't know how to use them or get along with people.

· · · · ·

Competitions are restricted within a department or region.

Pre-selection of a candidate through appointments to gain job experiences.

Eliminating candidates through screening for various reasons to support pre-selection.

Judging of qualifications by candidates not investigated.

Women who act like men are more likely to get promotions.

Board questions may favour certain candidates, reinforcing pre-selection.

Marking process of competition may be biased.

• • • • •

In my opinion, the Government's policy on equal pay for equal work is great. But to hire, for instance, women, simply because a quota is required, is ridiculous. All I can say is that if I owned a company, I would hire the best skilled people I could find. I would certainly not hire women or minority groups simply to fill in a quota.

• • • • •

Merit and job performance are very important factors to determine advancement. Personal feelings regarding an employee should not be allowed to be considered in job competitions. I also feel that the personnel department should have to be present on all boards so as to eliminate favouritism on boards. I also feel that if the employee for the job has already been selected by management that a competition should not be run. This costs the Government several thousands of dollars per year on wasted boards and truly makes all candidates feel "Why bother."

I feel much research should be considered in the advancement of both men and women in the public service.

• • • • •

My experience has been very negative. I only stay now because of pension concerns, but I would leave immediately if I found work in a company with a pension transfer agreement.

Initiative and ingenuity are seen as character bias. I now direct my creative abilities toward my private life and put nothing but bare minimum effort into this job. For this I come out with a "Superior" performance rating!

I feel I have done more to enhance my lifestyle and (family) income by assisting and facilitating my husband's career (outside the public service). Maybe other departments are better, but I'm almost too cynical now to bother trying to find out.

• • • • •

It seems that you have to know someone in authority to get ahead or even get in. I was lucky — I was at the right place at the right time and really did well on the interview. I was a term for approximately three years. But my luck seems to have run out. I've been in the same position for ten years.

Also courses really help to give you confidence and try for better jobs. A chance for secondment and acting is also a very good incentive for women who want to get ahead. Good communication with your superiors would help, but it is sometimes very difficult when it's a one way street. I also find that when you're good at your job they want to keep you there, so it makes it very difficult to get ahead. I work in a very limited environment, so job opportunities are very scarce. When there is a job opening everybody applies for it. So your chances of getting the job are slim, especially if they already have someone in mind.

Budget cut-backs also have an effect on advancement opportunities.

• • • • •

If a person has been judged (people in our department do a lot of this without really knowing the facts — gossip!) to be like this or like that, because of the gossip, the individual has been established as having a bad reputation, therefore when openings occur that individual won't have a hope in hell if the board members have "heard about he/she."

If an employer does not like an employee only because they just don't hit it off, he gives that employee a questionable or lousy appraisal without even considering if the person is really quite good at what he/she does. Something like this could screw-up a person's career very quickly. I believe that a lot of this goes on in the public service but employers would never admit to that.

• • • • •

I find it surprising and unfair that an individual can be assigned to an acting position yet is not eligible to compete for the position in question, i.e., SM acting in a DG position (EX-2) while the competition is open to EX-1 and above only.

I have also observed that those in "acting" positions seldom get the position once there is a competition. An acting situation seems to stifle advancement rather than improve opportunities.

• • • • •

I'm currently with DND. At the present time I have several supervisors — you can imagine the problems that I daily incur. Many of the lower level supervisors in DND would gladly accept more work and responsibility, but if they do they receive no recognition or raise in pay. I have a high school diploma, I am a graduate of technical college and two years of apprenticeship in refrigeration and air conditioning. When you apply for positions in the Government that ex-military are also applying for your chances are nil.

It is an unwritten rule in the Government that ex-military are given special consideration when applying to the public service. You can see how this becomes very frustrating for civilians.

This is not fiction but fact as I have personally witnessed this procedure time and time again. I have personally over the years accepted more responsibility and had my job description written to include these duties, but when it comes time for reclassification the support I need from my supervisors is non-existent.

The pay level and responsibility between military and civilian supervisors is far too wide and unfair. Many times we must train the military to be our supervisors, then they move on and we stay the same.

DND compared to other departments is often under-classified for its civilians and most certainly over-managed. The personnel department of DND over the years has turned to another branch of upper management. This quite often leaves the person feeling in a helpless situation and help other than from the union is non-existent. Overall the morale in DND is at an all-time low — long periods of negotiations for new work contracts, over-management, lack of support from supervisors, wide difference in military and civilian pay, military attitude towards civilians, and no chance of advancement or recognition for civilians have helped turn DND into a very cold atmosphere to work in.

• • • • •

Lack of real authority, poor morale in public service management jobs — this boils down to not being able to fire people who should be fired. This reality dissuades people like me from accepting a promotion to senior management. This difference in salary (about $7,000 year) is not worth the price of being required to put up with deadbeats and slackers. Please don't get me wrong — I believe most people work best with acceptance and support rather than threats and punishment. But if you can't deal with your hard core turkeys the organization and the people in it suffer badly.

Public service practice is to protect (and overprotect) employees — some of whom haven't earned it. The public service tends to turn itself inside out to make sure people don't lose their jobs. Some of this is very reasonable — I think people should have a reasonable degree of job security. On the other hand when we plug people into jobs just because they don't seem to have much else to do — you block promotional opportunities and the job doesn't get done very well. I have experienced this personally two or three times in the past five years.

Cliques of middle-aged macho managers — I have seen these cliques behave something like a dog pack — treating attractive women as a kind of personal trophy to be won. These people will compete with each other to see if they can get Ms. X to work with them on committee Y, to get them to go to conference Z, etc. In my view, these guys are pretty confused in their need for power and sexual dominance. I guess the less attractive women have to stay on the other side and don't get the special treatment including advancement.

• • • • •

No support for families, no adequate child-care leave, no positions which allow for flexible work schedule to meet family needs, no real development of useful skills, no opportunities to use skills and experience acquired. Senior women managers carry additional burdens not shared with male counterparts when both have children or are in the process of having children. When both parents work for the federal service some additional support should be given to help support and encourage healthy, happy, family situations.

Those people who do not have children have incentives and opportunities unavailable to working parents. My wife is a professional — (lawyer) with the civil service ... bilingual ... is not receiving/has not received any help from any one. She is underpaid, overqualified. Why, you ask? Lawyers are mostly men. The union is male dominated and older men at that and the Government is an ass.

• • • • •

... largest barrier to advancement in the public service is the staffing process itself. It takes far too long to staff positions — in most cases six months to a year and in some cases two or more years, particularly where reorganization and reclassification of positions is involved. Consequently, there are a lot of acting appointments, secondments, etc. This gives, I believe, an unfair advantage to those individuals when the competition finally gets completed. Secondly, for those individuals who are acting, because of the time usually involved, it puts a lot of pressure on them to win the job. Because of this assumption a lot of qualified people don't apply which is also a problem or disadvantage. Along with this aspect I would say that there are a lot of serious problems when at last positions are "boarded" etc. The situation now gives a lot of credit to the expressions "who you know" or the "old boys' network." Another major barrier to advancement is the current pay scale within the public service. With each advancement you get an increase in pay corresponding with an increase in job responsibility, duties, etc. However, a point is reached when you go above what is usually referred to as the "working level" within each group where the pay difference between the level you are working now and the level you will be going to is not worth the change. This is a major barrier to a lot of very qualified, top-notch people, who simply don't want to advance because it is not worth it.

· · · · ·

The public service is great at making up programs for promotion and developmental positions, but rarely does the average employee reap the benefits.

Sometimes you feel the more dedication you show the less likely you are to become promotable.

Sometimes the "squeaky wheel gets the grease." If you do not have that kind of personality you feel you lose chances that you may or should be entitled to.

If personnel is a department that offers a means to get promoted or seconded why have they not succeeded in responding or acting on my requests?

· · · · ·

A barrier I've noticed in my particular division (shift work) is a lack of co-ordination/communication between supervisors. This makes it very difficult for employees to effectively perform a job when each supervisor has different expectations re performance, how a job should be executed, employee requirements, etc. Therefore an employee's evaluation may vary according to which particular shift superintendent did the evaluation and how successfully an employee manages to figure out each supervisor's particular "nuance, requirement, etc." and then co-ordinate these expectations to "always be meeting the supervisor's interpretation of our job requirements."

A barrier other women have faced has been women with new children being placed in shift work positions when they have specifically requested to work "straight hours" for a short period until the baby can more easily be adapted to the parent's absence.

I have personally experienced and have had several other female officers relay to me experiences of sexual discrimination in the workplace. My experiences have involved not being taken seriously, having my enforcement decision/action either questioned or taken over when a male officer (same rank and experience) who made the same decision was not questioned at all. (My original decision/action was eventually determined to have been the correct one to take.) I have also been in meetings and discussions with all male supervisors where I and the other female officer I was with have been completely ignored and if we made suggestions they were not listened to — only to be brought up again later by one of the male officers and this time listened to and acted on. During such a "meeting" the other female officer and myself were referred to as "the girls" while the other (male) officers were referred to and acknowledged by name. My female colleague and I discussed the experience with very open minds and determined that we were experiencing actual discrimination and were not "jumping the gun" to cry "discrimination" because we're women. This is just one example reflecting similar experiences I have witnessed or heard of women having to deal with — on top of dealing with the regular challenges of the job and officer/management relations.

I have however, found that most fellow "male" officers I work with are very fair and treat others according to performance not sex.

· · · · ·

The barriers I face are:

The "buddy system" — employees get acting positions because they are in with the supervisors.

Knowledge — too much emphasis is placed on knowledge in the competition process. If an employee is "groomed" for a position, it is virtually impossible to beat his/her knowledge hence I lose. The emphasis should be placed on one's ability to learn and perform.

Dead-end careers — because I am working in a dead-end job in a dead-end office, I need a government with a policy to rotate me into different departments. There isn't any getting out.

· · · · ·

I was promoted to an office in Ontario following a competition for a PM-4 position.

I find that Ontarians are more receptive than the Québecois to the promotion of women. As a bilingual Francophone I have been made very welcome in an English environment.

· · · · ·

My wife was in an acting CO-3 position for a year. Her actual level is AS-2. Despite the fact that her performance was excellent, she was not considered for an acting CO-1 position because she does not have a university degree. This is a flagrant example of an obstacle to advancement.

· · · · ·

Mobility between departments is practically non-existent.

If directors general of personnel would consider the resumés and requests of employees in other departments, they could expand the options for women. The transfers are often limited to those within the same department. The nature of the work of the department may not particularly interest candidates who would fit in much more easily in another department.

• • • • •

I would have liked to see nurses assigned to patient care units based on their therapeutic specialties and desires, rather than random assignment ... as a result, I have had to sit out one year on an interesting, but less desirable unit, biding my time to request a transfer to a more preferred unit (where I feel I am better qualified) and even that transfer is unconfirmed and may not be forthcoming. Transferring in this institution can be quite troublesome for many nurses and has even caused union involvement.

• • • • •

I would hope that the level of performance in your job will speak for itself when being considered for advancement, and the best person shall overcome all barriers. However, women are not thought of as equals, in general, either by your co-workers, your manager/supervisors, and hence not by the people (public) that you have to deal with. Accordingly, I feel women have to always be on guard so as not to be tripped up and give others a chance to ridicule or criticize you — a black mark never to be forgotten. Should a woman receive a promotion, she is, it seems, further alienated by her male dominated co-workers. The perception or feeling is that she is undeserving of the position, especially since they didn't get a promotion. I feel the greatest barrier to a woman's advancement is the co-workers, managers, and supervisors' willingness to form opinions on hearsay/one side of the story/rumours, etc. They are so ready to judge you on every move you make and everything that you say. Unfortunately, the manager that writes up your appraisal does so by judging you not by what he sees directly, but by others' perceptions of you, which could be detrimental.

I guess one word of advice for women working in a male dominated profession is, don't ever be more efficient than your superiors, as they will tell you to be less efficient and brown-nose a little bit more. Just do your job, be polite, and don't say anything unless specifically asked for your opinion and even then think about what you're going to say very seriously, so it can't be used against you. Most of all, enjoy your work, or get out.

I really enjoy my job for the most part, now that I have learned (the hard way) what is to be expected of me in order to get ahead.

Thank you for this opportunity.

• • • • •

Because management is male dominated, boards past the PM-1 level are presided over by men who, I believe, base decisions on factors external to the posted position, i.e., personality.

Women seem to populate the entry and lower levels of job classifications whereas men dominate the senior levels and management positions. This suggests to me that employment equity has managed only to improve the mean numbers of female employees and has not resulted in an overall shift, sexual balancing, of the department as a whole.

I believe that women have to work twice as hard for recognition.

As well, contrary to the official position advanced by the federal government I do not think I have been given opportunity to progress as a member of an aboriginal group who is as well qualified or better qualified than many of my peers.

· · · · ·

Unfortunately, Customs and Excise continues at this time to be discriminatory towards women in managerial capacities. This starts at the PM-2 level and the number of female managers is incredibly low. As an example we have 13 senior managers and only one is a woman. I realize that there are many women who are not truly interested in managerial positions. However, those of us who do must try and fit in with what I call "the boys' club." In other words I'd better learn to play squash or racquetball soon!

Another comment I would like to make is that many senior managers keep to their "old school" ways which makes it tough for women to be looked at seriously for management positions. These managers still think women should be married and at home with the kids. I hope that perhaps in future generations, men will change their attitudes and get more with the times. Women are here to stay and we will get ahead.

· · · · ·

My experience has shown me that the manner in which candidates are selected for acting positions is definitely a barrier to advancement. Rather than choosing by merit, choices are made by either the popularity of the individual and if they will be "yes" people for the egos of the boss. Another factor has to do with whom one knows. This is a very strong factor. Consequently, some employees are groomed from day one of being employed.

Both males and females in the public service are very much aware that assignments are made arbitrarily and that they are used as a basis for grooming favoured employees. So, the principle of fairness to all employees is grossly compromised. While it is true that employees can

Women are here to stay and we will get ahead.

grieve the assignments, sometimes employees are fearful of the back-lash such an action can and does have on any future advancement for them. They remain silent, become twisted and bitter and show great disinterest and disloyalty to management. Such behaviour as unco-operativeness and gossip fills the work environment with negative energy. Another observation is that the same employees are always selected to attend courses for on-the-job training. Many "excuses" are given by management.

What needs to be in place is a "selection criteria" that is known to all employees so that the grounds for selecting employees for assign-ments or job-training are clearly defined. Assignments then can be seen to have been earned by merit.

My own experience regarding opportunities for advancement has been good. However, the promotions were part of a plan, they were the result of actions taken by me including grievances and threatening to quit. Middle-level management gave me support but it was difficult getting decisions through personnel and senior management.

In my opinion one of the significant barriers for advancement in the federal public service is the arbitrary academic requirements for spe-cific positions which are dependent upon the occupational group selected for that position. However the occupational categories are limited and do not represent the current range of jobs in the public service. This is very evident in Environment Canada. The traditional occupational groups used for environmental protection positions included engineer (ENG), biologist (BI), chemist (CHEM), and engi-neering technologist (EG-ESS). This limited selection resulted in artifi-cial constraints regarding who would qualify for a particular position. In reality not all positions required a particular academic degree such as an engineer, biologist, or chemist. Environmental protection is a multi-faceted responsibility and each position, professional and techni-cal, requires a blend of those traditional academic pursuits. Also, due to the occupational group structure the organization chart was devel-oped with an engineering side and biology side and others such as chemists, geographers, etc.

The ultimate result of this is limited opportunity for individuals to find promotions within the organization. Also, there are virtually no transfers within sections of the department. In my own case, I was not eligible to fill my supervisor's position because I had a degree in chem-istry but my supervisor's position was classified as a biologist.

In another case a hard-working and talented engineering technolo-gist (EG-ESS) was frustrated for years in not being able to advance even though he was assuming greater technical and professional responsibilities.

The EG-ESS occupational group is very restricted in capacity for advancement. Generally, higher level EG positions require supervision of two or more subordinates. The current public and political demands to downsize the public service result in less and less of these subordinate positions. This presents barriers for people currently classified in occupational groups such as EG, PM for which the classification standards are largely based upon the number of subordinates. The area of "academic equivalency" based upon experience should be reviewed by the Public Service Commission and Treasury Board.

· · · · ·